This Is
Not My Life

A MEMOIR OF
SISTERHOOD, SUSPICION AND
STARTING OVER

LAURA BURKETT

This is Not My Life:
A Memoir of Sisterhood, Suspicion, and Starting Over

Copyright © 2025 by Laura Burkett. All rights reserved.

Published by:
Sevan House Publishing

Hardcover ISBN: 979-8-9986322-1-1
Paperback ISBN: 979-8-9986322-0-4

Cover Design and Interior Layout: Fusion Creative Works, fusioncw.com
Author Photo: Olivia Vickers, Alchemical Image

Printed in the United States of America

First Edition

This book is dedicated to my late mother, Janice Marlene Burkett.

I will be our voice, Mom.

Table of Contents

The Dysfunctional Family Photo

AUTHOR'S NOTE: This is a true story based on my personal experiences. To protect privacy and for legal considerations, all names, including my own, have been changed, and some identifying details have been altered. However, the events, emotions, and experiences described represent my actual lived experience.

CHAPTER 1

How's Your Sister
and Fidel Castro?

My sister ran away to Puerto Rico when she was 15 because she got a bad perm. How magnificent is that sentence? I am going to say that I am 99.9% certain that I am one of the only people on Earth who can truthfully write that. I find that very cool.

It was the mid-eighties, and Camille was in her Stevie Nicks phase. She loved her. She would listen to her music constantly, often singing along to the same song over and over again. I can still see her standing in the bathroom with a white towel wrapped tightly around her, hanging her head upside-down, blow-drying her hair with the radio perched on the sink blasting Fleetwood Mac. One of her favorites was *Landslide*:

Well, I've been 'fraid of changin'

Cause I've built my life around you

But time makes you bolder

Even children get older

And I'm gettin' older, too

I can still hear her voice blending with Ms. Nicks every time I hear that song. It's kind of funny that at 15 she connected so deeply with the adult lyrics. But Camille was the proverbial "old soul." Camille emulated Stevie Nicks' style…right down to the hair. She had frosted her dishwater blonde hair and gotten a perm. I must say, there was an uncanny resemblance to the legendary singer-songwriter. She had pulled off the look. Camille decided that she needed additional curl, and I can remember her badgering our hairdresser mother to give her another perm.

"Camille, no, it will fry your hair. It's colored and I just permed it not too long ago."

They went around and around about it for hours. This was nothing new in our house. Camille was entirely too persistent when she wanted something for my mother's personality to ever resist. My mother could be a mule but Camille was definitely the bigger ass in the family. By that evening, there she was in the kitchen with the rods in her hair smelling up the house with the perm solution. Now, here's a shocker, her hair was fried, absolutely fried, even by Stevie Nicks standards.

This hair catastrophe was now very clearly my mother's fault. At least that is what I caught by the screaming and hissing that ensued in the house after Camille saw her hair in the mirror. I was only 12 years old at the time and witnessed how completely innocent my mother was in this, but once again, Camille won. They went to our regular hairdresser who informed Camille that short of shaving her head, she had about a year of re-growth before her hair would be normal again.

"I can't go to school like this! They'll torture me!"

That statement did ring true. We went to school in a middle-class, wannabe upper-class suburban area that bred the girls unnaturally pretty and unusually mean. *Yep, they're gonna torture you*, I thought, but didn't dare say it out loud. I didn't dare say a lot of things out loud. I was a silent spectator to insanity in my home.

My dad allowed Camille to stay home from school for a few days but told her she was going to have to return after the weekend. The discrepancy in our treatment from our parents was evident to me. I was never permitted to miss school. I would have to cough up a lung and go, "Look Dad, see…this is my lung. Can I please stay home?" Camille… bad hair…stays home…hmm?

The news of her return did not go well with my sister. I can remember a lot of her running around the house screaming. My mother would try to calm her and she would throw herself at the wall, pounding her body against it in an attempt to hurt herself. I can even recall a tense moment between us where she was threatening suicide.

"I swear, Lana, I will kill myself if they make me go back. I can't be seen like this. I will get one of Dad's guns and blow my head off!" she told me through tears in her bedroom.

I sat quietly on the other bed and listened to her, trying to remain calm, but I could feel my heart thumping in my chest.

"No, you won't," I said with a bratty tone.

But as soon as I left the bedroom, I walked around the house making sure that my dad didn't have any of his guns out. Then, the scariest thing of all happened.

She got calm.

I heard my parents frantically whispering early Monday morning. I got out of bed to listen from the top of the stairs to try to make out what they were saying from the foyer below. I peeked into my sister's room to ask her what was going on, almost knowing what I would see – an

13

empty bed. She was gone. I lingered at the top of the stairs waiting, waiting to be told what had happened.

Instead, my father yelled up the stairs, "Lana, time to get up for school!"

I ducked my head out of the stairwell to escape detection from spying. I knew better. I didn't ask. I never asked. Where my sister was, why did my sister act the way she did, how did this always keep happening? Those questions just weren't asked. She was who she was. And, at that particular moment, who she was – was gone.

My father had gone into the deposit bag in his briefcase and found a note in the place of a couple thousand dollars that read, *Sorry about taking the money, Dad. I'll be back when my hair grows in.* My parents flew into a panic, and I went off to school. I hadn't coughed up any lungs after all. My mother immediately called the police, and they told her to relax and that she was probably at a friend's house.

My mother replied, "Sorry, sir, but you don't know my daughter."

He sure didn't.

My sister had called a cab in the middle of the night and taken it to the airport. Armed with cash, she approached the desk and asked for a ticket to *anywhere warm, where I don't need a passport to get to.* Off to Puerto Rico she went. My sister did look a bit older than her 15 years, but I will always wonder why the ticket agent didn't stop a young girl with fried hair and cash asking to go *anywhere.*

It was not very 15 for Camille to call a cab in the middle of the night. It was not very 15 for her to take an airplane to a foreign place alone. It was *very* 15 of her to check into an expensive hotel once she got there and blow through all the money she had in a few days.

Meanwhile back in the States, the attached ones at least, my parents were going crazy trying to find her. They had absolutely no idea where she had gone. They knew she had one friend, Kristen. They called her and grilled her and her parents about Camille's whereabouts. When they determined she was not there my father devised a plan. We had a family member with the ability to tap phones. So, my father had my sister's friend's phone tapped. (*There's one of those sentences again.*) It didn't take long before the collect phone call from Camille to Kristen to come in: "*Puerto Rican operator, will you accept a call from…Camille?*"

My father came through the front door of the house and slammed it hard behind him. I was sitting on the couch in the living room with my feet perched up on the coffee table watching Guiding Light, my favorite soap opera as a kid.

He stomped into the room, looked at me, and said, "Puerto Rico. Your sister's in Goddamn Puerto Rico!"

I bit the inside of my cheek without breaking my gaze from the soap opera and said, "Yep. That sounds about right."

I looked at my dad and nodded and went back to watching Reva Shane sleep her way through every male member of the Lewis family, which, considering my life, didn't seem so preposterous. My sister was a perfectionist. She never did anything halfway. She would, of course, run away in the most dramatic fashion possible.

My dad and grandfather booked the next flight to Puerto Rico to find her.

News of her escapade traveled fast through our small town in the suburbs of Pittsburgh.

The next day I went to school and a not-so-bright wrestler nudged me in the hallway and laughed. "Hey, how's your sister and Fidel Castro?"

"That's Cuba, you jerk!"

"Your sister's in Cuba?" he dimly replied.

This was my first experience of being "the sister of the girl that...." Until that point, I was just Lana to the public at large. I later had a friend tell me that he thought everyone to some extent always sees themselves as the person they were at 12 for the rest of their lives. At 12, I was the "sister of the girl that..." and he was right, that was a definition I carried for a very long time.

When my father and grandfather hit the streets of Puerto Rico armed with pictures of my sister, they quickly realized it could not have been a worse time. It was Spring Break, and the island was full of college students looking roughly the same age as my sister. She had now been gone for two weeks.

Puerto Rico, like many resort islands, is deeply divided in classes. There are the very rich and the very poor and little in between. The hotels for tourists were often far removed from the reality of the island. My father knew how much money my sister had taken and considering the length of time she had already been gone and her proclivity to spend, they didn't bother checking into a hotel and opted to go straight to the impoverished areas of Puerto Rico to find her.

They had assumed the worst, that she had run out of money quickly and would be forced into the streets to fend for herself as a helpless child. They were only half right.

Camille was not in the streets of Puerto Rico. She had blown through the cash she had lifted from my father and was wandering through the gift shop attached to the hotel lobby crying, dragging her suitcase with her last bits of cash in hand. She took her toothpaste and a box of cereal to the gentleman running the shop to check out.

He took one look at her and asked, "Are you a runaway?"

She nodded yes. The shop owner had a daughter close to Camille's age and he took mercy on her.

"What is your name, young girl?" he asked, smiling a bright white smile made brighter by his deeply tanned skin.

"I'm not telling. You'll call my family, and I can't go home – not until I look better," she replied, tugging at her curly hair.

He cocked his head to the side in confusion.

"I am not sure what you see wrong with your hair. But I can't have you just leave here alone. It isn't safe out there."

He scratched at his wiry black hair and thought.

"How about I allow you to stay here?" He pointed to the back room of the little shop. "But you need to help work the register when my daughter returns to school after the break."

"Yes, yes. Thank you…" She paused, struggling to know what to call him.

"Luis," he said, extending his hand to shake, "and now I must have something to call you."

She thought for a moment and responded, "C. You can call me C."

And, just like that, my sister went from a lonely, scared runaway with frizzy hair to an employee with friends (still with frizzy hair) in Puerto Rico within days of arriving.

17

It was growing dark and my father and grandfather decided to check into a hotel to drop off their bags and resume the search in the morning. As they entered the lobby of the hotel, my dad caught something out of the corner of his eye. A fuzzy head was quickly ducking behind a counter. He made his way to the shop and leaned over the counter.

Camille looked up at him and began to cry. "Sorry, Dad."

That was it. They had found her on the first day!

My father called my mother and let her know they found Camille unharmed and said, "Puerto Rico is beautiful! We are going to stay a couple more days."

Overhearing the conversation from my usual spot on the couch, I was simultaneously relieved and irritated.

She runs away to Puerto Rico and gets a vacation out of it! I thought angrily.

Camille returned home without punishment. They switched her to a private school to spare her from the abuse of the other students due to the stigma attached to her getaway and of course, the bad hair. I was left in the public school district to be teased about it. To be fair, I never told my parents that I was receiving the ribbing that was meant for her. Over time the story became more legendary than it did scandalous.

I was able to turn it around on them. "Yeah, she ran away to Puerto Rico! Isn't that the crazy, coolest thing you've ever heard?"

Somehow that crazy reputation bled on to me. If I was the sister of the chick who ran away to Puerto Rico, surely, *I* had to have inherited some of those bold, daring, and flat-out crazy genes. The truth was that

18

I hadn't. But bold, daring and even crazy was not a bad perception for other teenagers to have of you. So, I took it, even if it didn't belong to me.

Now, as the sole survivor, I take her story. It doesn't belong to me, but in many ways it does. Her life defined my own. To tell you of my sister's death and all the strange circumstances surrounding it, I first must tell you how she lived. I don't think it will make sense otherwise. The only way I can tell that is through my eyes, her little sister, her only sibling. This was not my life, this was not my death. But I was there. The sister of the girl who died. The sister who lived to tell the tale.

CHAPTER 2

The Phone Call

It all started with a phone call. Maybe this is the way it really happened or maybe this is the way I now remember it in my head, but the phone rang in such an ominous way that it let me know that this call was different. This call was going to change everything. It was December 28th, 2002 and I was at my home celebrating my husband's birthday. Christmas-time babies always get the short end of the stick, but Frankie's mother always insisted we make his birthday separate and special. So, as the tree lit up my living room, we gathered with his big, Italian family to mark his 34th birthday.

I could hear the phone ringing from the kitchen, but I was seated on the couch in the living room in conversation with my husband's aunt Katie. I paused for a moment to hear if my husband had picked up the ringing phone. He had.

I could hear his deep voice answering, "Hello."

I lifted my finger up to Katie requesting her to wait a minute as I listened.

He was yelling, "What? What? Who is this? I don't understand you!"

He hung up in confusion and came walking to me from the kitchen clutching the cordless phone. "Hey, I think that was your dad, but he was screaming so loud I couldn't understand him."

I looked at him puzzled as I usually did. "So, you hung up!"

I was irritated at the lack of logic in that decision but was interrupted by the phone once again ringing. This time, I snatched the phone from his hand and answered.

"It's your sister, it's your sister, oh my God, go to her house now! I just called her, and Lee said she had a massive heart attack! She's not breathing! She's not breathing!" my father wailed. "I'm at camp, we're on our way. Go there. Go there now, Lana!"

None of what he had just said to me made sense.

My sister was only 33. She was perfectly healthy. I had just spoken to her earlier that day. Yet, I had no doubt about the urgency of his plea. I had not one ounce of doubt. I set the phone down and ran up the four stairs of our multi-level house to my 18-month-old son Aaron's room, as my husband followed. I fell to my knees next to his empty crib and clutched onto the cherry wood bars.

Frankie appeared behind me aggressively barking questions. "What? What?! What's going on? What is your damn dad screaming about?"

As I told him I began to pull the bars apart, cracking one slightly. "It's Camille. Something bad is happening. My dad says she isn't breathing!" was all I could get out.

He looked at me in disbelief.

"Oh, I'm sure she's fine. What did your dad say to you?" His tone was condescending, and it angered me.

I didn't bother to answer him and got up and ran back down to the entry closet. By this time, his entire family had gathered quietly in the living room.

I threw on my coat and shoes and, ever the good hostess, said through my tears, "I apologize. I have to go."

The streets were incredibly bare as I frantically made my way to her house. I only lived five minutes and as many turns from my sister's home that she shared with her second husband, Lee, his 12-year-old daughter from a previous marriage, Ashley, and Camille's three small children from her first marriage, Mitchell, Gabriel, and Nicole. It had just begun to snow rather hard, and my headlights were reflecting off the thick white flakes and making it hard for me to see. There were only two stop lights between our homes, and I had the luck of both of them being green. I wouldn't have stopped for them, anyway. Nothing could stop me from getting to her, to her children who I imagined had to be terrified.

No matter how fast I went, it felt like it was taking years to get there. I sped up more, breaking through the thick snow that was overpowering the windshield wipers. I was driving almost blind through the streets I grew up on. I knew those turns and roads so well that I could drive them with my eyes closed, yet the town I was raised in lost all signs of familiarity at that moment. It, in the blink of an eye, had become a ghost town to me.

I was going nearly 75 mph when I glanced up at a large digital clock that sat in a little plaza right before I had to make the right hand turn off the main road into her quiet residential neighborhood. It was 7:27 PM. I hit the right turn fast, fishtailing and briefly losing control of the car. I took the car to a complete stop sideways in the middle of the street. Just then I thought, *you better slow down a little. Your parents can't lose both of their children tonight.* I shocked myself with that thought and right at that moment I felt the horror to come. My stomach tightened and I knew my sister was gone. No matter what the death certificate says, for me, that was the moment I lost my sister, sitting in my car in the middle of the road at 7:27 PM on December 28th, 2002.

As I was making the final turn to her home, my father called again.

"Are you fucking there yet Lana!"

"Dad, Dad! Stop yelling at me. I'm going as fast as I can!"

I can only imagine that for many families that have experienced a sudden loss this description may be familiar: the phone ringing and the subsequent panic, tears, and disbelief. Unfortunately, for my family her death was only the beginning. Her death would prove to be as complicated as her life. Fitting, I suppose. I continued the drive to her house at a more reasonable speed and thought the words that I would repeat over and over again in the years to come, *this is not my life.*

CHAPTER 3

Paging Dr. Freud

My father was an angry man. He was a former Marine and a Vietnam Veteran. Mom said he came back from the war a different person. But my sister and I never got to see what version of him left to fight a war, only the one that would come back to wage one on us.

He worked so much that he was often reduced to the smell of lingering cologne in the air. And when he was there, he stole the oxygen from that same air and made us just long to smell only his cologne. My dad never left and he financially provided for us. I think we all held onto those things like that was all that mattered.

He would lie about things unnecessarily, pathologically. I learned that the hard way at seven years old when my dad told me he knew Michael Jackson and I went to school and told everyone. They laughed at me, and I shrunk in humiliation. I don't know how my sister and I fully processed his pathological lying. It was unspoken our entire lives. It was a shared eye roll between the two of us, a cringe. We just always knew that we couldn't believe much of anything Dad told us.

As we grew older, his lies started to include us. I got accepted to a simple, small college and my dad told people I was going to an Ivy

League school. My sister got her private pilot license, and my dad said he was the one who taught her to fly. Those were the lies that ran deep through both our veins. Those were the lies that imprinted on both of us, one simple truth:

You aren't good enough as you are.

In the starkest contrast, my mother downplayed her own achievements and stayed silent on ours. My mother couldn't stand when other parents would brag about their kids. She would just smile and nod. She was honest to a fault. My mother was one of those people who would tell you if your butt looked big in those jeans, but in the nicest way possible.

Honey, I notice that when I wear jeans, they make my bottom look quite wide.

She was raised primarily by a single mother in a poor area of town, but she carried herself with a prim English refinement. Every single day of her life she woke up, put on a full face of makeup, and got "dressed for the day," even when she had nowhere to go.

Girls, you need to never allow yourself to look terrible in front of your husband.

As we aged, my sister and I appeared to the world as girls who were high maintenance – no hair out of place, fearful that we would be spotted at the grocery store without makeup. But behind it were my mother's words that our appearances meant something. It meant Dad would stay. Fresh-washed, bare faces were things only for us to see in the mirror.

We weren't good enough as we were.

My father, at my mother's urging, followed his dreams and went with all of us in tow to chiropractic school. That decision gave us a comfortable life and afforded my mother the ability to stay home with us. My father was a traditional guy, and I really don't think he would have accepted another setup. But he would often befriend other women in the professional world and speak of them in such high regard that it would clearly hurt my mother. He would push me and my sister into pursuing high career goals in such a way that said without saying, *Don't be like your mother.* He did not have much respect for her, and it was apparent to me and Camille.

"Shut the fuck up, Marlene. I'm talking!" was often heard in our home.

But he would also tell us how much he loved our mother. Therefore, love in the absence of respect became our normal.

My dad was a bull, and my mom was the China shop. Meeting at only 14 and 16, they grew up together. What also grew was a level of codependence that both baffled and irritated me and my sister. My parents never had a handle on exactly how they were talking to or treating the other one. My father was big on telling us not to disrespect our mother on the heels of telling her to shut up. She, on the other hand, had too much respect for him. She wouldn't defend herself because he was "the man of the house." She pouted and forgave, pouted and forgave.

There was a lot of, do as I say, not as I do, going on in our house. It was a weird dynamic for Camille and me to watch. We could see it, but they could not. It often led to Camille and me believing that when it came to parenting in our house, the lights were on, but no one was home…but us.

Camille, as much as she resented my father, took on his anger and I favored my mother's personality to deny, defend and avoid. When Camille and my father would clash it was thunderous. During one particularly bad fight between them, my mother pulled me into one of the bedrooms and locked the door.

"Lana, let's pray for them."

"Okay, Mom."

We knelt at the side of the bed as the screaming and breaking of things ensued outside the door and prayed to God, "Please don't let them hurt each other" in unison as the screaming and slamming of things hurt us all.

Camille refused to back down to my father and it would often lead to him chasing her around the house. She would slam one of the bedroom doors in his face and lock it. He would punch through the door. Eventually, we ended up with solid wood doors throughout the house, which I'm sure my mother preferred because they were prettier. Although I had endured a few beatings at my father's hand they never escalated to the levels of my sister and father's fights. The trick was to lie still and take it. If you saw him take off his belt, it was time to be quiet. Camille was never one to lie still.

My father always had a motorcycle. He would sometimes ride me to school on it. Then, out of the clear blue, he would abandon his "you must be on your deathbed to miss school" attitude. We would whiz by my middle school without stopping.

"You missed the turn, Dad," I would yell over the engine.

"Hell with it. Let's just keep going!" he would yell back and rev the engine.

He would drive us through the countryside and then stop and get ice cream and take me fishing. I was never quite sure why he would do that. Maybe because I was the baby, and I was growing up and he wanted to seize the moments he had left with me. Maybe because he just wanted to blow the day off and didn't want to do it alone.

At the time, it didn't matter why to me at all. I would do anything my dad wanted to do just to hang out with him. I needed his approval and acceptance. Camille did not and somehow in a world where I felt like I couldn't compete with her on any other level, getting Dad's approval was the one place I could shine. The trick, you see, was to just pretend to like what he liked and do what he wanted to do.

Camille also picked up my father's language and could swear with the best of them when she was angry. It was such a contradictory sight. She looked like a Barbie Doll, but if she got angry, the sewer could pour from her mouth. My mother hated all of this, especially the language.

She would say, "Joseph, we're raising young ladies, not truck drivers."

He would of course say, "Shut the fuck up, Marlene."

Added to this amazing mix of dysfunction in my household were my maternal grandmother and her husband, Bill. My step-grandfather, Bill, had suffered multiple strokes, and my grandmother was still working and unable to care for him on her own. So, they came to live with us. The strokes rendered Bill paralyzed on one side and he lost his ability to speak.

The only word he was able to mutter was, "Goddammit."

My mother said this was odd because he did not cuss much when he was well. Besides the Goddammits, Grandpa Bill had a few compulsions because of his strokes. One was to stand and flush the toilet all day long if you let him. Another was to open the front door and blow

29

his nose on the bushes next to the front door. Another was to pee on the bath towels. My favorite was his compulsion to steal my grandmother's cigarettes, which he was forbidden, and try to light them off the stove. Being paralyzed in his left arm, he could not feel the fact that he had set himself ablaze.

This would lead to moments where my friends would turn to me and say, "Lana, your grandpa's on fire." (There's one of those sentences again.)

I found my grandparents so amusing at 13. I would play little games with Bill. I would ask him funny questions, to which his reply would always be, "Goddammit."

I would giggle and he would giggle. "Goddammit."

My grandma would get in between me and my sister's fights by throwing shoes at us when we were acting up. I found that funny, too. She was like a gunslinger and had amazing aim. Camille would be mouthing off and Grandma would reach down, pull off her shoe and whap. I found that really, really funny. My sister, on the other hand, was now nearly 17 and found snot in the front bushes, flying shoes, pee-covered towels and flaming grandfathers not nearly as funny as I did.

There was a story that Camille loved to tell everyone about me. She would tell it well into adulthood with a sense of wonder and amazement.

"Lana never cried as a baby," she would tell people with the tone of a proud, but confused mother. "She would have a shitty diaper and just sit there and smile. No one would even know she needed anything unless you smelled her." She would laugh. "She would just sit there in shit all day if you let her."

What she saw as this amazing testament to my go with the flow nature, I saw as something entirely different...my role.

CHAPTER 4

Superheroes

I straightened out my car and made my way through the residential neighborhood to Camille's house. I knew the streets well, as she had bought a home after her divorce from Sean only one block away from our childhood home, the house with the snot in the bushes. Lower Burrell is where we spent much of our childhood and the small town that we both had vowed to get out of had a familiar draw to it as we aged and had children of our own.

I pulled up to her house and the combination of headlights, streetlights and porch lights lit the night sky. I veered my car off to the side of the road and ran through the mix of neighbors, medics, and law enforcement officers to her door. Her house was a lovely two-story home filled with antique furniture and redone hardwood floors. Sean and Camille divorced the prior year as amicably as any couple could ever. Rather than an official settlement, he bought her a home and a car. He let her know that, any expenses the kids incurred, he would always be there for her, as he always had been.

I opened the front door to see a police officer standing with his back to me at the bottom of the stairs. He turned his head in what seemed like slow motion and I immediately recognized him. His ice-blue eyes connected with mine and he gave me a look of pity that, combined with the sound of the paddles still shocking Camille echoing from upstairs, made my knees buckle. I had seen this look from him before. My legs failed me and I dropped to the floor.

From the ground I listened intently to the sound of the shocking coming from the upstairs bedroom. I shuddered every time I heard the paddles hit her chest.

I began to mumble to myself, "Stop. It has been too long. It has been too long."

I was calculating the time in my head from the phone call to my drive over. If they were still trying to revive her, if she wasn't breathing all of this time, it was just too long. I was sobbing on the floor when I felt a sharp tug on my arm.

The officer was pulling at my left arm and firmly telling me, "Pull it together. Her children are in the next room. Go comfort them."

"Okay," I muttered and breathed deeply while standing up.

When I stood up, I spotted Lee, her second husband of only 18 months, for the first time standing in the hallway. He was wearing a red turtleneck with a black nylon pullover, blue jeans, a baseball hat, and work boots. I scanned him up and down, but we didn't speak. Something wasn't right with what I was looking at, but I didn't have time for that now.

I walked into her living room filled with lovely, oversized furniture flanked by bookshelves. A Tiffany lamp lit on a table to the left. Sitting on the couch in ascending order of age were Nicole, a raven haired, full-lipped version of her mother at two years old, Gabriel, a scrawny but scrappy five-year-old, and Mitchell, a meticulous ball of stress by seven years old. Nicole was in a pink nightgown clutching a blanket. Mitchell and Gabriel were in matching Spider-Man pajamas, blue bottom with red shirt. A spider web was silk-screened on the front of the shirt and between the arms was a flap of fabric that when their arms were raised revealed a web. I recognized them because my boys had the same ones.

They looked so scared and confused. Their eyes widened as I walked into the room.

"Hi, guys." I said.

"Hi, Auntie Lana," they said in unison.

They weren't crying or moving around at all. They just sat there still on the couch. Mitchell sat on the arm of the couch with his head down. I knew that because he was the oldest, he had the best idea about what was going on.

"Mitchell, your mom is going to be okay," I leaned over to tell him.

He lifted his head, and his eyes welled up with tears. "You promise?"

"Yes, Mitchell. Auntie Lana promises," I said with certainty in my voice, but not in my heart.

I should not have said that, and I really believe that Mitchell still resents me to this day for lying to him. My family and friends have tried to tell me differently, but I wish I could take back some of that fake certainty. I knew in my heart everything wasn't going to be okay. I knew at that moment that there were no superheroes going to save the day.

"Is Mommy going to be with Alan?" Mitchell asked.

"No, Mitchell," I reluctantly replied.

It had only been six months since we had all experienced a similar scene. I couldn't wrap my mind around how it could all be happening again. How could this all be happening again? I pulled Mitchell into my chest and peered back into the ice-blue eyes of the police officer who was there that day six months prior. He stared back at me as we both read the same words going through our heads: "How is this happening again?"

This is not my life.

CHAPTER 5

Daddy Issues

Camille's hair had grown back in what seemed to be Mach speed by the time she was 16 and it looked better than ever. It was a paler blonde, straight, and hung down to the middle of her back. She had outgrown the Stevie Nicks phase and had slimmed down even more. My father wanted to get his private pilot license and had taken Camille with him. She fell in love with flying and quickly became one of the youngest females to perform a cross-country flight. There was a big article in the local newspaper about it. I was now "the sister of the girl who flew airplanes." She now carried herself with a certain air of confidence due to that. Up until that point, she had made her way through different pursuits: piano, cheerleading, etc. But when Camille found flying, she found her niche and it showed.

Camille spent a lot of time going back and forth between our home and a small, rural airport to fly her beloved planes. On one particular trip with one of her girlfriends, they were pulled over by the police. Camille was not yet 17 and the cop was 32 years old and married, but they began an affair. When the affair came out, rather than prosecute the officer, everyone including my parents buried it to avoid a scandal. I watched my parents rationalize that she was the pursuer in the relationship and that as long as it ended quietly, it would be best for all involved.

I was now called, "the sister of the girl who was having an affair with a married cop."

Then, there was Sean. Sean was Camille's flight instructor. He was a soft-spoken 30-year-old man and brilliant when it came to airplanes. He worked as an airline mechanic and could build airplanes from scratch. Camille quickly became as enamored with Sean as she did the airplanes. She would spend endless time at the small, privately owned, grass landing stripped airport in rural Pennsylvania. There was a small clubhouse where all the pilots would convene. It was a little, old wood paneled room that always smelled of fuel and coffee.

It was a funny sight to see Camille sitting around there, a young, petite blonde girl with Sean and five other guys in their fifties and beyond talking "airplane talk." If you didn't fly airplanes, you could only understand every 27th word they said. But she loved every minute of it and could talk shop with them like a pro. They would have big picnics, and all the pilots would open their hangars and bring their families. By this time, my father had bought a small Cessna, and our family became regulars at the airport. I would pal around with the airport owner's grandson, and we would ride a little scooter around the airstrips, often crashing it. It was peaceful there and I could see why she liked it.

Sean was aware of my sister's crush on him but would not acknowledge it. She was 13 years his junior and he was a good guy and found it inappropriate. My family had gotten to know Sean very well through our time there at the airport. It didn't take Freud to understand why Camille continuously circled around much older men. But Dr. Dad didn't seem to get his role in that.

"I have no idea why Camille keeps chasing these older fucking men," my dad said to me on one ride out to the airport.

I just raised my eyebrows and shrugged back at him. "Yeah. No clue. Weird."

Camille began openly dating Sean because there really was no stopping her, anyway. From that point on, no matter what role Sean played in Camille's life – instructor, lover, friend, husband, ex-husband, father to her children – he was always there. Through all her ups and downs in life, he became the horizon that she looked for to gain her bearings and fly straight again. He was her constant until the end.

But no man, in my eyes, ever compared to Alan. He was the first guy I remember Camille bringing home in high school. He was a 6'4" captain of the swim team with dark hair and sweet eyes. He was handsome and funny with a self-deprecating humor that endeared him to all. He was the only child of older parents, and he seemed to relish in the craziness and fullness of our family, even the snot in the bushes! He participated and added to my family's bickering and bantering and could match wits with us. My mother adored Alan and thought of him as an extra child. The boy she never had.

I liked Alan and Alan liked me, too. At 13, I guess I had a tiny crush on him, but it was more like he was this really cool big brother. Unfortunately, Camille got bored of their romantic relationship quickly and Alan got put in the box where Camille put all age-appropriate men.

CHAPTER 6

I Have Never Seen an Ambulance Drive That Fast

We had lost touch with Alan over the years. He had married and moved to Florida and had two children. Camille had run into him at the grocery store years later, as she was going through her divorce and moving back to our hometown. Alan had gone through a divorce, too. They stood in the aisle and shared "loser" stories. They both viewed their divorces and re-entering the singles scene in their thirties as single parents as a huge failure. But they were together with their shared wits able to find the humor in it.

She had brought him to my house shortly after they had re-united.

She called me from her cell phone and said, "Come outside. I have a surprise guest for you!"

I stepped out the front door and there he stood smiling at the end of my driveway in khaki shorts and a navy blue polo shirt. He had put on a little weight and was now wearing wire-framed glasses, but when he smiled, I instantly recognized him.

I was seven months pregnant with Aaron at the time and I waddled down the driveway to hug him. I was just so excited to see him.

He took one look at my belly and laughed. "Wow! You look beautiful! You're so grown up."

"Alan, I'm a whale," I sighed.

I was a bit embarrassed that, after all these years, he was seeing me looking bloated and pregnant.

"Oh, no doubt!" He laughed. "You're a fatty, but that will pass, kid." Then he rubbed at what was the beginning of a dad bod belly and said, "At least you have an excuse."

He made me laugh. Alan always made me laugh.

We would meet up at Camille's house and drink coffee or iced tea. The kids would go play happily in the playroom downstairs and we would sit in the kitchen and gossip or complain and mostly laugh. I didn't tell my husband that Alan was there as much as he was. Frankie was an extremely jealous guy. There was absolutely no reason for him to be threatened by Alan being around, but I had learned from experience with him that if I didn't want our little get-togethers to be ruined, I was better off omitting the frequency of his presence.

I spent the sunny June days, prior to Camille's death, at the pool at Brackenridge Heights Country Club with my boys, Michael and Aaron. BHCC is set on a hillside with a lovely view of the Allegheny Valley. The clubhouse was a rustic, brick house and was the site of many of my family's showers and events. It was an unpretentious club by country club standards.

Michael was taking daily swimming lessons and Aaron, still too young, splashed around with me in the adjacent baby pool while Michael took his lessons. Michael's swimming lessons usually ended by 2:00 PM. Aaron was ready for a nap and so was I. We packed up for the day and began to make our way home. I made my way through Natrona

Heights and began to cross the bridge to my home. The windows were rolled down and I could hear an ambulance in the distance. I looked to make sure it wasn't coming up behind me but saw nothing. As I proceeded across the bridge, I spotted the ambulance coming from the opposite direction across the bridge. I have never seen an ambulance go so fast and commented on that to the boys.

I've never seen an ambulance drive so fast!

I could hear the house phone ringing as soon as I pulled into the garage. I was too busy pulling Aaron, now sleeping, out of his car seat and carrying him up the stairs to his crib for his afternoon nap to immediately answer. The phone hung up and no sooner began to ring again. This happened at least four times until I was able to get Aaron settled and get to the living room where the phone was docked. I glanced at the caller ID, and it showed 42 missed calls. I went from being irritated to being alarmed. The phone rang again before I was able to check the source of all the missed calls. It was my father.

"Alan is dead, Lana. He drowned in your sister's pool. He's dead," my father shouted at the top of his lungs.

"What in the hell are you talking about?" I screamed. "You mean he's hurt?"

"No, Lana. He's dead. You should go to your sister now!"

"When did this happen? I saw the ambulance. I saw the ambulance. It was speeding so fast. I bet it was him in there. He's not dead Dad, he's hurt. You're lying to me."

Please let him be lying this time. Please.

"Lana, he's DEAD!" my father yelled, now sounding angrier.

I screamed, "No" from a place inside of me that I didn't know existed. I scared poor Michael with my wail, and I scared myself.

I called my husband at work sobbing, "Oh, Frankie, please come home. Something horrible has happened. Alan has somehow drowned in Camille's pool."

"What the fuck, Lana. I can't right now. I'm working."

"Frankie, please."

"I'll get there when I get there. Plus, if he's dead, what's the point of going anyway?"

I felt such deep hatred for him at that moment.

Almost an hour had passed, and Frankie had still not returned home after my urgent plea. I was furious with him. He and his father owned a painting company. I knew they were working a job locally and that if he wanted, he could have been home in minutes. I was convinced he was taking his time on purpose and ran to the neighbor's and asked if she would sit there with the children until Frankie got home and she agreed. As she made her way across the lawn to my house, Frankie pulled in the driveway.

I told her, "Thanks, anyway."

He came walking nonchalantly up the stairs and I just glared at him and grabbed my keys and went.

I pulled up to Camille's house on that bright sunny afternoon to see Mitchell and Gabriel wrapped in swim towels sitting by themselves on the front porch. They looked completely pale and in shock, clutching their towels and rocking back and forth. The ambulance was gone, but one police car remained parked in the driveway and my father's Tahoe was parked on the road. There was also a man with a notepad standing in the front yard, who I later found out was a journalist from the local newspaper. Looking at this scene should have made me realize the reality of the situation, but I still believed I was going to see my sister and she was going to tell me Alan was hurt, not dead. Dead still made no sense to me.

"Where's your mother?" I asked the boys, but they didn't answer my question.

Mitchell looked up at me and said, "Alan went to Heaven."

Just then, a police officer emerged from Camille's front door. As he pushed open the screen door my eyes connected with his ice-blue eyes.

"Alan went to Heaven," Mitchell repeated.

The officer continued to look at me and pursed his lips together when Mitchell spoke. Camille came out behind the police officer looking exhausted but composed. The second she saw me, she flung her body at me and all of her composure fell.

"I can still smell him!" she sobbed, wrapping her arms around me. "I can still smell him."

Indeed, I could smell the distinct aroma of men's cologne that had transferred onto her from her futile effort to lift the lifeless Alan out of the pool.

As we hugged and cried together on the front porch, Mitchell stood up and started pacing back and forth repeating, "Alan went to Heaven. Alan went to Heaven."

As much as Alan being dead was unbelievable, so was the way he died. My sister sat and recalled the day's events to me. The month prior, Lee had installed a four-foot above-ground pool in the backyard of Camille's house and decking with stairs leading down to it. It was a sweltering June day and Alan called to come over. He was complaining that his father had started dating again so soon after his mother lost her battle with cancer. Camille told him to come over and cool off in the new pool to get his mind off things.

Camille went out to the pool. She was painting her toenails poolside and making the kids wait for Alan to get there before they could get into the pool. Alan must have let himself into the front door as he appeared at the top of the stairs.

"Kids, Alan is here! You can jump in now," Camille stated.

Alan came down the stairs and, without saying a word, he fell face first into the pool. He was on his belly doing a dead man's float. Camille told the kids to jump on him. She thought he was kidding around. The boys jumped on him, but he didn't move.

Mitchell said, "Mommy, he's sinking."

Camille jumped in the pool after him, half thinking that if he was joking around it wasn't funny. Plus, she was messing up her freshly-painted toenails. She got a hold of him and pulled him to the surface and rolled him over. His eyes were wide open, and he wasn't breathing.

Chaos ensued. My sister was screaming for help at the top of her lungs. She and the two small, adolescent boys were pulling with all their might to get him out of the pool for Camille to perform CPR on him. Alan's 6'4" frame was too much for my 105 lb. sister and two little kids. She was screaming so loud, she drew the attention of her neighbor. The kind, middle-aged woman jumped in to help. But it was too late. The ambulance came, the same one I saw speeding across the bridge, but Alan was gone without explanation.

Alan's funeral was fast and sad on so many levels. It was all going to be done on one day, the viewing and the burial. My husband refused to go with me.

"I don't know that guy," he said angrily. "You just go."

I sat alone in my car in the parking lot trying to compose myself. My tears seemed to anger my husband, so I would cry every time I got away from him. I stepped out of my car and ran into an old gray-haired man with sweet eyes, Alan's sweet eyes. It was Charlie, Alan's father.

"Hi. I'm Lana, Camille's sister."

"Oh, I know you. Alan would talk about you all the time. He would always say you were the sane one." He laughed. He grabbed my hand and said, "Let's do this."

Charlie became my friend as quickly as Alan had.

We walked into the funeral home, and I was struck by how empty it was. My family, Charlie, Alan's ex-wife and her new husband with Alan's children, a young girl Alan was casually dating, and a few guys I didn't know. This was a young guy. He was only 35 years old. Where was everybody? It hit me that we were really all that Alan had. We were his family. I walked with my mother to his casket. She leaned over and wrapped her arms around him, laying her head on his chest. She stood back up and stroked his cheek.

"You sweet boy," she cried and turned to me. "You know why I loved him so much, Lana?" She continued with no answer from me, "Because he always seemed to enjoy us, just *enjoy* us, never judge. Never him. He just seemed amused. I am going to miss…" Her voice trailed off as she stared at his face.

"Is that a bump on his forehead?" I asked my mother as she continued to just look at him in the casket. "Did he hit his head?" I pointed at a slight red mark on his forehead covered by makeup.

"I don't know. I don't think so," my mom replied, never breaking her gaze.

We both stood in front of him for a while. I was just trying to memorize his face.

My dad and I stood alone together at one moment during the viewing.

"I'm worried about her." He nodded his head in Camille's direction. "I just don't know how she's going to deal with this."

Camille stood across the room in a black, sleeveless, shift dress with white piping around the arms. She leaned against the wall staring in the direction of Alan's casket looking frail and dead behind the eyes.

"You need to be there for her, Lana," my dad said, reaching out and holding my hand.

"I will, Dad. I promise."

Just then Lee walked by and my dad's eyes narrowed a bit.

"And she has to deal with that asshole and his daughter…too much stress for her…too much. I just don't know how she's going to deal with this. You need to be there for her."

"Dad, I will," I repeated, a bit annoyed.

CHAPTER 7

The Rascal's Rejects

My sister and my husband despised one another. He was in every way not her type of guy and definitely not her pick for my life. He judged her openly for the way she behaved, especially in her marriage to Sean. She found this so repulsive. Frankie had a drinking problem and trouble keeping a job. My sister's life was raw and exposed with every mistake she made becoming public. Frankie was better at putting up a front. Even the lovely home we lived in had to be negotiated to a rent-to-own scenario because Frankie lost his job right in the middle of the mortgage process. Of all the things Camille hated about him, it was the fact that he was hypocritical that drove her the most nuts. Camille did not like fake.

They both equally didn't care that I was stuck in the middle of this. During the early days of my marriage to Frankie, I came home one afternoon and my mother was there watching my newborn son while I was at work. My mother and sister had been arguing back and forth on the phone. My sister was angry that my mom was there helping babysit my child because she needed help more. She always needed help more than I did in her mind. My mom kept hanging up on my sister and she kept calling back because she wasn't done yelling, yet. Frankie had gotten home from work early and intercepted her call.

"Camille, don't call my house screaming and hollering like this," he barked and then hung up.

I walked in from work right at the moment he was slamming down the phone on her.

The phone rang again, and I pleaded, "I don't know what is going on, but please don't answer it, Frankie."

For all of their hatred of one another, Camille and Frankie shared one trait, their ability to "go there" in an argument. You know those soft spots that you avoid to not permanently damage someone? When they were angry, neither of them would side-step those spots. In contrast, they would jump up and down on top of them.

The argument between Camille and Frankie quickly turned vicious. He told her that if she hadn't had parents with money, she'd be in a trailer park somewhere and she told him he was a drunken bum that as soon as her sister smartened up would be gone. The screaming went back and forth for what seemed like forever. He would yell and hang up. She would call back, yell something, and he would hang up again. My mother and I just sat as spectators until finally I secretly turned off the ringer on the phone. My husband sat shaking with anger on the couch for a moment with his head down, thinking.

He looked up at me and proclaimed, "You are never! Do you hear me? NEVER, to see your sister again! She will never be around our children! I am done with her and so are you! Or I'm done with you, too!"

I did what I was trained to do. Listened to him.

I missed a lot during that year. Camille had rapidly re-married Lee, a local electrician who she met, ironically, through my husband. I sat in the parking lot across from the church on the day of their wedding to catch a glimpse of her and the children. I slouched in my car and cried as I watched them all happily exit the church. My sister and I had fought terribly throughout our lives, but it was unheard of in my family to miss such a milestone. I didn't like or trust Lee at all and I equally disliked his 12-year-old daughter, Ashley. Something about Lee did not sit right with me from the first time I met him, even before he started dating my sister. I had witnessed first-hand how terribly Ashley treated my sister and her two boys, especially Mitchell. I wasn't happy about her decision to marry him, but if Frankie hadn't forbidden me to see her, I would have attended the wedding.

After Alan's funeral, I returned home to a pouting Frankie. He refused to even acknowledge where I had been. I smoothed out my black dress and walked up to him as he slouched on the sofa watching television with a beer in his hand.

"Aren't you going to ask me how I am?" I asked.

"Nope. Don't care."

I stood for a minute nodding my head, trying to fight back the words that years of conditioning told me to battle back.

"Well, prick…I do care. You don't have to like my sister. But you aren't keeping me from her anymore. If you don't like it, there's the door."

He picked up the remote and motioned with it like he was going to throw it at me. Gritting his teeth he lowered his arm, pointed the remote, and changed the channel.

I left the room thinking the channel wasn't the only thing that had changed.

My family was able to return to normal once I stood up to Frankie, albeit our normal. Camille and I were free to talk and hang out. I would get some eyeball rolling and pouting from Frankie when I would do things with her, but I learned to just ignore it.

In November, Camille called to arrange an impromptu fifth birthday party for her son, Gabriel, and suggested that we meet at a local indoor playland. We met at Rascal's, one of those God-awful, money-pit, noisy kid traps. My mother, father and grandmother would meet us there after my father got off work. I arrived on time and Michael and Aaron immediately removed their shoes and started climbing through the indoor maze of tubes and slides. Camille came in about a half hour late and visibly irritated. Camille didn't explain why she was late but glanced over at a pouting Ashley and did the combination head shake and eyeball roll. The children quickly jumped into playing and Camille shook off her irritation and generously went to buy tokens for the arcade for each child.

Besides one other family with two kids, our crew were the only customers in Rascal's that evening. It was easy to spot my father carrying a large white box containing the dinosaur-themed cake, coming through the front door with my mother and my grandmother. My mother and grandmother made their way towards our group, but I noticed my father being stopped by the young man from behind the concession counter. My father was toe-to-toe with the chubby employee with brown slicked back hair pulled into a tiny ponytail. The next thing I knew, my father turned on his heels with a dead look on his face and walked back out the door.

"I think something's up," I informed Sean.

Sean went to investigate the problem. He found my father sitting in his Chevy Tahoe with the cake riding shotgun.

"The little prick won't let me bring the cake in. I worked all day! I don't need this shit. I'll be out here with the cake," my father grumbled.

Camille hadn't noticed the missing cake and father, yet. The always reasonable Sean went to the young man to try to figure out the issue of the cake before she caught on. Apparently, the smug young man was the owner's son. He informed Sean that if we were having a party there, we needed to inform them first and order the cake through them. Sean apologized for the error on our part and offered him $20, surely more than the profit they made from the forced ordering of the cake through them. The young man refused and insisted that the rules were the rules in such a nasty and snide manner that it ruffled even the ever-calm Sean.

As Sean was whispering to me what was going on, Camille finally noticed there was something amiss and demanded to know what it was.

Sean filled her in, and little Gabriel overheard and started to cry, "I want my cake. I want my cake."

The combination of Camille already being irritated by Ashley mixed with her low tolerance for bullshit and her violently protective nature when it came to her kids was the perfect storm. Camille stood up in a fury and made her way to the cocky young man behind the counter like a tsunami. Sean and I gave each other a knowing glance. This was not going to end well.

It all happened too fast. In the time it took for Sean and me to glance at each other and get up to follow her, it was too late. She was already hurdling the counter and jumping on the man's back with the guy's little ponytail firmly grasped in her delicate fingers. She looked so tiny wrapped like a spider monkey around the chubby six-foot young man. He tried to make his way to the phone on the wall with her riding on his back and as he grabbed the phone receiver, she ripped it out of his hand and started hitting him in the head with it.

Sean flipped the counter gate to pull her off him and as he broke free, he ran to the back of the concession stand and grabbed the phone. "I'm calling the cops!" he screamed, visibly shaken. "You are all to leave immediately!"

So, my entire family, including six children and a little grandma on a cane, got kicked out of a child's playland. (There's one of those sentences...again.)

Camille and my parents made a clean getaway, but I was unable to get the kids strapped into their car seats in time to beat the police. The furious young man had followed us all outside and was standing behind my car to block my getaway. When the police officers exited their cars and walked up to the both of us standing in the dark parking lot, he fingered me as his attacker.

"It was her. She attacked me!" he squealed.

"It wasn't me, you twit, I'm the sister of the chick...never mind," I thought to myself.

There was a rush of explanations that clearly amused the cops a little. They were trying to hold their belts and look profoundly serious, but I could detect a slight smirk on both their faces. A trace of amusement ran across the ice-blue eyes of one of the officers. I realized that if I just calmed down and spoke softly and apologetically, I would be okay. I was sprung from my police confinement of the playland parking lot with the agreement to never return there again, which was an easy promise to make!

Everyone had re-grouped at Camille's house. The children ran downstairs to her playroom, seemingly unaffected by the evening's drama. Camille got on the phone and ordered pizza.

My father took the cake out of the box and placed it on the table. "Here's your fucking cake!"

We all looked at each other and laughed until tears were streaming out of all our eyes.

CHAPTER 8

The Hospital

Lee jumped into the back of the ambulance with Camille, and I was left to watch over her children. I quickly called my best friend, Jillian, who lived nearby, to sit with them.

"Are you kidding me, bud?" she replied when I told her that something was very wrong with my sister.

"I wish I was."

All I knew was that I had to be with my sister. Jillian arrived and I raced to the nearby hospital alone. I didn't feel emotionally equipped to deal with this all by myself, but I had no choice. My parents were still returning from their camp two and a half hours away. My husband was no one I could turn to for support. It was a lonely drive to the hospital.

I arrived at the hospital and made my way quickly to the emergency room waiting area. Lee was there with his friend Tony, a friend from Fox Chapel who Camille had spoken about. I found it odd that he could have arrived there so quickly, but after a quick introduction, I insisted on seeing my sister. A nurse informed me that they were stabilizing her for Life Flight. They were going to transport her by air to a hospital in Pittsburgh that was better equipped. They took me through the curtain to see her and it was a horrific sight. She was seizing uncontrollably, and the convulsions were causing her to lose control of her bowels. The room smelled putrid. They asked me if she was on any street drug.

"Of course not!"

My sister never touched drugs and barely drank alcohol. They asked me if she was taking any laxatives. I had no idea and couldn't understand how that would be relevant. They kept asking me questions, but all I could do was stare at her arms. She was posturing. Rigidly turning her wrists in and curling up her arms. I knew from my brief stint in chiropractic school that it was a sign of neurological damage.

Tony and Lee sat on one side of the waiting room and whispered to one another. I felt so awkward and unwelcome. I paced the floors between the waiting room and the room where Camille lay waiting for my parents to arrive. Through the glass automatic doors, I saw my parents walking swiftly toward me. I stood inside the doors relieved that they were finally there.

My mother ran straight at me and grabbed both my wrists and looked me dead in the eyes. "Lana, tell me. Tell me it is not that bad." She whispered. "I know you will tell me the truth."

"Mom, Mom…" I began to cry. "It's so much worse."

I barely got the words out of my mouth before my mother let out a wail that will echo through my soul for the rest of my life, the howl of a mother losing a child. Her knees gave out beneath her, and she clung to me to stop herself from hitting the ground. I held onto her limp body in my arms. Of all the tragic moments, this is the one that still wakes me up at night. It was the moment a daughter broke her own mother's heart, the moment a mother told another mother her child was dying, and the moment I first spoke out loud what I knew in my heart, my sister wasn't coming home.

"Mom, she's still alive. It's nothing you want to see. But they will let you see her."

With the words that her daughter was still alive, my mother sprang up and followed me to her room.

My father had already passed us and was standing near her bed when my mother and I entered the room. He was watching her, examining her. My mother just went to her head and cradled it. Thank God, by that time the nursing staff had given her something to stop the violent convulsions. She lay still with her hands still curled up. My father moved her hand, lifted her arms, lifted the white sheet, moved her feet, and pulled open her eyelids to see her pupils. All the while, my mother kept cradling her head and stroking her hair.

"Joseph, how bad is it?" my mother asked.

My father, in his typical callous tone and always one to respond first with anger, replied, "Marlene, she's fucking gone!" and stomped out of the room.

My mother looked up at me with a helpless look in her eyes for a moment and continued to stroke Camille's hair. I stood in the corner of the cold room and silently watched them tend to her in their own ways. I couldn't speak. My head was racing with one thought.

This isn't real. This is a bad dream. Wake up, Lana. Wake up.

But I didn't and I wouldn't. Nobody was waking up from this.

This is not my life.

CHAPTER 9

The Dysfunctional Family Photo

"Wake up, Lana. Wake up."

Camille shook my shoulder as I slept peacefully in my canopy bed.

As I opened my eyes to see her standing there with her stained sweater I had ruined, I didn't have enough time to shield my head as she punched me square in the eye. She grabbed me by my long, blonde hair and dragged me out of the bed to the ground to take another swing at me.

Thud

"Girls! What are you doing?" Mom yelled from downstairs.

"Nothing, Mom. Lana, the klutz, just tripped getting out of bed."

Taking and touching things that didn't belong to me was a genuine issue in our home. It was the source of many intense arguments between me and my sister.

This is one of those points in this story where she would be chiming in, "You were a brat, and you wouldn't keep your hands off my stuff. It's that simple!"

It wasn't that simple to me. Camille and I both had blonde hair and blue eyes, but that was where the similarities stopped. She was nearly four years my senior and as an adolescent, I idolized her. Even amidst her crazy antics, she always seemed so put together, so pretty, so perfect.

I was a mess. I had inherited my father's height and my mother's skin. So, I had grown to 5'8" by the sixth grade and was as white as a sheet except for the freckles. My mother wouldn't let me cut my hair until I was 13. So, I had long, white-blonde hair that grew below my waist-line. I had also hit puberty earlier than most girls and had begun to develop, which led me to believe I was fat compared to the other girls who were still built like boys.

Camille had received the genetic lottery of my mother's petite frame and the deeper complexion of my father's Italian ancestry. I felt like if Cousin It and Casper had a kid it would have looked like me, and having a sister that looked like Malibu Barbie made me even more insecure. There was a big part of me that thought if I wore her sweater, her perfume, her shoes, I could be her. This NEVER ended well.

We shared a Barbie Dream House located in my bedroom next to my bed. Camille took great care to cut my mother's plush pink towels to give the cardboard house the finishing touch of wall-to-wall carpeting. I, on the other hand, would use the Barbie elevator as a convenient way to get rid of my gum before I fell asleep for the night. I would lie in bed and pull the elevator string up, put my gum on top of the plastic elevator, and let it drop. She would hit the roof when she found the dried gum on it. I would carefully play with the Dream House trying to make sure everything was back in place before she noticed. But she always did. The fake plush carpeting always gave me away. She could tell by imprints on the towels that things had been moved, and it would always lead to a verbal or literal smackdown.

"Stop touching my stuff!!!"

Despite our vastly different body types and even though I had a closet full of clothes, I would sneak into her drawers and take her things. One summer day, I squeezed my 5'8" medium-framed body into her small light pink, petite, capped-sleeved summer sweater. I came out of the house to meet my best friend, Reese. We were going "out" for the night. At 13 years old in Lower Burrell, that meant walking the main drag in between McDonald's and the corner 7-Eleven.

She took one look at me crammed into that sweater like a summer sausage and screeched, "Jesus, Lana, would you stop taking your sister's clothes? You're going to get grounded AGAIN and ruin my summer!"

I didn't listen and we went "out."

"It'll be fine. She'll never know. She's out all night, and I can sneak it back into her drawer before she gets back," I replied confidently, with no reason to ever be confident.

Remember how I said this NEVER ended well? Reese and I were walking down the main drag and someone, apparently unhappy with their chocolate ice cream cone, threw it out the car window. Reese looked at me standing there in horror as the cone had splattered right in the middle of my chest.

I stood with my arms at my side and chocolate dripping down my sister's sweater as Reese part yelled, part laughed, "Great! Just great! There goes the summer!"

Camille would weep when she found her ruined items buried like artifacts under my bed. (Under my bed was where I always hid everything. This proves that I in no way inherited her craftiness.) She never did buy my doe-eyed, "but you always look so beautiful, and I wanted to be like you" excuse. Maybe it was because of her own insecurity, but it really was the truth. Nevertheless, I was always sorry that I caused her so much grief, even if I didn't show it. Our dual insecurities were a trait that we did share, and we both felt we earned.

There's a family portrait that hangs in my parents' dining room. Camille and I referred to it as the Dysfunctional Family Photo. The day of the photo shoot was classic Kennedy. My mother scheduled the picture to be taken. This is the time when most families would show up, get their picture taken, and go home. Things never ran that smoothly for us.

On that particular day, 13-year-old Camille wanted to wear jeans instead of a skirt with the frilly dusty rose blouse my mother had put out for her. She argued that you really wouldn't be able to see the jeans if the shot was only going to be from the waist up. My mother argued that the jeans would show in the picture and that Camille would look so much prettier in the skirt. My father argued that she would wear the skirt or get her ass beat. Dad won the battle but lost the war.

We arrived at the studio as the stunning Kennedy Family. Two blonde-haired, blue-eyed children, a handsome doctor father, a beautiful mother still in shape and attractive in her thirties, and the family pets, Wally the loveable Lhasa Apso and Shingo the cross-eyed Siamese cat. The photographer could not see what was really coming at him that day.

The photographer seated my mother and father on a wooden bench, and stood Camille behind my father and me behind my mother. My mother was to hold the dog on her lap and my father was going to cradle his beloved cat. That was the photo that was planned for the day, but certainly not the photo that emerged.

The skirted Camille had plotted her revenge, and the dog and cat seemed to be in on her plan. The dog, usually calm, wouldn't stay on my mother's lap and quickly jumped down and raised his leg on the photographer's tripod. He was out of the picture from that point on. The cat, in the distinct Siamese voice, began to shriek and growl at the photographer and scratch up my father. Camille, well…she just refused to smile for the picture. My father, when he caught onto the fact that she was scowling every time the photographer would go to take the shot, would fire a backhand towards her and bark, "Smile, dammit!" which, shockingly enough, had the opposite effect.

Finally, I think we just settled for the best shot we could get; my father with a fake grin and crooked tie holding a ballistic cat, my sister behind him scowling, my mother sitting tall and pretty, and me in a white dress with tiny polka dots smiling obliviously. This was my normal, after all.

CHAPTER 10

The Long Ride

The air transit arrived to take her to the downtown hospital, and Lee, my parents and I all jumped into my father's Chevy Tahoe for the trip down. The staff at the local hospital told us not to rush. They said there would be a significant amount of time before we would be permitted to see her once she arrived in the helicopter. We made our way downtown. My mother and father were in the front seats and Lee and I in the back seat. No one was talking. No one asked Lee what had happened. After all, we didn't have to. Lee immediately started making phone calls, one after the other.

"Camille had a *massive heart attack!*" he would proclaim. "I went in the shower and came out and found her on the floor."

He would hang up the phone, dial another number and repeat the entire story again verbatim.

"Camille had a *massive heart attack!* I went to the shower and came out and found her on the floor."

He seemed oblivious to the fact that my mother would tighten her shoulders each time he recounted the story. My father would look at my mother and grip the steering wheel. After the sixth phone call, I found myself wanting to grab his phone out of his hand and throw it out the window.

I fought the words back down in my throat, "Shut the fuck up, Lee! Shut up!"

Instead, I leaned my head against the cold glass, and the lights from the traffic coming in the other direction in the dark night blinded me and took me back in time.

My sister refused to attend a summer trip with her friends to Ocean City when I was 15 and she was 18. Of course, she changed her mind around 11 PM and somehow convinced my parents that I should go with her. My reaction was not much different than when they would leave her to babysit me.

Are you CRAZY, Mom and Dad? She doesn't actually want me to go with her. She just doesn't want to drive alone. So, she is forcing me to go to be her ride down wing woman. Chances are, she will dump me off the second we get there and go off with her friends for a week. I will then wander off and get sold into sex slavery and you will never see me again. This seems like a very unwise parenting choice, and I hate you all.

Well, that is what I thought. Of course, I said nothing, smiled, and packed my stuff, essentially knowing the chances of me coming out of this unscathed were highly unlikely.

I have been blessed with a pretty keen sense of direction, and from the many beach vacations we drove to with our family, I was certain Camille had got on the Turnpike going the wrong direction.

"Camille," I meekly asked, "Are you certain we're going the right way?"

"Yes, I believe so."

She was in a decent mood. I was optimistic. When we hit the Ohio sign after traveling an hour and a half in the wrong direction and she completely melted down, my optimism died.

"Fucking great! Great!" She screeched the van over to the side of the road. "This just added three hours to the trip, and I am already exhausted. Forget it! We aren't going."

"Okay, Camille. I'm fine with that. Let's go home." I was relieved to not have to face a week of fending for myself.

"I'm too tired to drive," she said, like the words coming out of her mouth weren't ridiculous. "So, you're going to have to drive back home."

"Um…Camille. I don't have a driver's license."

"Then don't get pulled over."

"It's the Turnpike, at night, Camille. And I don't have a license."

"For God's sake," she mumbled and began to crawl out of the driver's seat and back to the back couch of the conversion van. "You'll be fine. Don't be such a baby."

I slid over into the driver's seat and took her place. I was panic-stricken at the wheel. The dashboard lit up and the van sat humming, waiting for me to take control.

"Oh my God, Camille, I seriously can't drive," I cried out.

She came flying back up from the back of the van and wrapped her arms around the front seat, grasping each of my hands.

"STOP being a baby! One hand goes here." She slapped my right hand on the wheel in the 3 o'clock position. "One hand goes here." She slammed my hand into the 9 o'clock position. "The pedal on the right is to accelerate, the one on the left to slow down! Now GO!"

On the word go, she released the van into drive and we coasted out onto the Turnpike.

The road was bare in the midnight hour, all except for large trucks. I was 15, unable to drive and holding on for dear life to the 3 and 9 o'clock positions screaming every time an oversized truck blazed by me in the passing lane laying on their horn because I was going as slow as I possibly could.

"Speed up, asshole!" Camille yelled from the back of the van.

She was sprawled out on the back couch of the van actually trying to sleep through this.

"I'm scared, Camille! I screamed back as another big rig blew by wailing his horn at me.

"Stop being a baby and drive the van! Your screaming is making it impossible to sleep," she yelled back, putting the pillow over her head.

I drove as many miles as I could possibly stand with my legs trembling and my fists dripping with sweat holding onto the wheel for dear life. A huge tractor trailer passed me and the draft from it caused me to shift to the right. I overcorrected and cut over to the left lane almost hitting another truck. He laid on his horn and held it. I started screaming again.

"Oh, for Fuck's sake, Lana!!!" Camille screamed from the back of the van. "Pull over!"

I was crying as I pulled over to the gravel area at the side of the road. By this time, Camille had flung herself up into the passenger side of the van. I looked down ashamed.

"I'm sorry. I tried," I cried.

She looked at me with irritation that was only mixed with the smallest trace of compassion.

"Whatever, you're a baby. Switch seats with me."

We slid over the center console, swapping places without exiting the van.

I stared out the window at the passing cars fighting back the tears. I wasn't crying because of the scary drive I just made, I was crushed because I felt like I disappointed her. She needed me and I couldn't come through for her. I WAS a baby. The cars whizzed by and stung my eyes and made the tears harder to fight.

"Camille had a MASSIVE heart attack. I was taking a shower and came out to find her laying there." Lee repeated it for the 100th time.

I let her down. I wasn't there for her when she needed me, I thought with my head still pressed against the cold window. Hearing him repeat the story again, oblivious to my father tightening his fists on the wheel and my mother tensing her shoulders, infuriated me back into the present moment. I lifted my head off the glass and turned to him and just stared at the side of his head as he talked. Dead-faced, staring at him. Not moving. Staring more. He finally took the hint and put the phone back in his pocket.

CHAPTER 11

Music and Booze

I began writing music at 12 years old out of laziness more than talent. I was required to practice for an hour every night with my mother listening from the other room. So, I had to play something. I would always hum little melodies that I heard in my head and rather than practice Bach, I would try to pull those melodies out of my head during my required time at the piano. One night, my mother heard me tinkering around with one melody and asked what I was playing.

I admitted that it was something in my head and she proclaimed to my surprise, "It's beautiful! Keep going."

I was certain she was just saying that, but I took the melody to my choir teacher, Mrs. Wilson, for confirmation. Again, to my surprise, she agreed with my mother. She went further and asked if I could put words to it. My family had dinner out that evening and all of a sudden, the words came to me. I wrote them on the nearest thing I could find, a cocktail napkin. I took the napkin into school the next morning and plinked it out for Mrs. Wilson. She asked if we could teach it to the choir for the next concert. Just like that, I was a songwriter. My one true thing of my own and I loved it.

Camille had her airplanes and I had my piano. We had found our own ways to escape that were as different as we were. For her, older men and airplanes numbed the pain; for me it was music and booze.

The one bright spot of being "the sister of the chick that" was that as I grew into my teen years, nothing much shocked my parents. To me, it seemed like if I wasn't hopping an airplane to some island, I was able to fly under the radar. To Camille, I was getting away with everything. One evening at my home, Sean and Camille were sitting on the couch watching a movie and could hear giggling and laughing coming from outside the house. It was me and a friend coming up the front walk. We came bursting through the door stumbling, slurring, and laughing.

Camille whispered to Sean, "She's drunk."

My friend and I ascended the staircase. My mother came out of the kitchen and asked Camille and Sean, "Was that Lana?"

Just then, they heard, "kerthunk, kerthunk, kerthunk," something falling down the stairs. My mother, hearing the noise, moved to the base of the stairs. The falling object, a can of beer, fell right at her feet. Camille turned to Sean, grinning like the Cheshire Cat.

Her smile said, "This is it. She's going to get busted. I get to watch. My life is complete."

My mother picked up the can of beer and yelled, "Lana Shae! What is this?"

I came down the stairs acting as sober as a heart attack to face her.

"Mom…that is a beer…there were kids drinking it at the party I was at tonight. Which we both know is very bad! I did not trust that if I didn't take the beer from them that they wouldn't just go ahead and drink it once I was gone."

I self-righteously grabbed the beer from my mother's hand and went marching back up the stairs with the beer in tow!

My mother turned to my sister and Sean and said, "She's such a good girl!" and walked back into the kitchen.

Camille looked at Sean, deflated, and proclaimed, "I hate her."

I continued to write music for the choir all through middle school. In high school, I wrote my class's graduation song. In college, my father agreed to finance an album of my original compositions. But he also told me, "there's a reason they call them starving artists" and persuaded me to keep music and writing as a hobby and "get a real job."

Eventually, marriage, children, and work got in the way of any dreams that I had of being a musician, but those melodies never left my head. I would write through a lot of distinct phases in my life. By 29 years, the lyrics of those years gone by lived on little scraps of paper stuffed inside my piano bench. Camille asked me that December why I had stopped writing.

"Oh, I haven't!"

I opened my bench and my heart to her by playing some of my stashed songs to her over the phone.

"My God, Lana, what are we going to do about this?" She was crying. "You can't give up on your dreams! I won't let you."

"Okay," I said sarcastically. "How?"

Well, so you just want to be a female songwriter? Right?"

"Yes."

"All right, who's the top female songwriter right now?"

I thought for a moment. "Diane Warren."

"Call her."

I giggled at the silliness of it, but knew that if I didn't, she would.

She immediately got on the internet and found the phone number for Diane Warren's production company and read it to me over the phone.

"Okay, now hang up and call her. What's the worst thing that could happen?"

I knew she would just keep hounding me if I didn't, so I hung up the phone and stared at the number for half an hour. I dialed Diane Warren's production company, True Songs, and reached an automated system. I just started pushing combinations of numbers to try to reach someone's extension.

A woman finally answered on the third ring. "True Songs, how may I help you?"

"Is Ms. Warren available to speak to me?"

"What is this regarding?"

I just began to babble. "I'm a songwriter, but I've never really pursued it in any meaningful way. I'm going to be 30…I have kids…I just want to know that I tried…I just lost someone close to me and I feel like life is too short…" I unloaded on this poor woman.

Unbelievably, she was so incredibly sweet and understanding and began to give me some advice and direction. She told me about the importance of being published, how often I should be writing, and most importantly how to start.

"Look," she said, "In March, there is an NSAI Convention in Nashville. Go to that. It will really help you."

I didn't want to tell her that I really didn't write country music and that I had no idea what NSAI was, so I took her advice, thanked her, and hung up. I googled NSAI and realized that it stood for the Nashville Songwriters Association International. Every year they had a four-day conference that would have publishers and established songwriters present to give advice and even listen to and critique your music.

I called Camille back and told her all about the progress I had made in just an hour of honest effort and about the NSAI Conference.

"Oh, we're going!" she replied.

"How?"

"I don't know, but we're going."

Two hours later she called me back. "Okay. We're going. I called Dad and told him about it, and he said he always wanted to go to Nashville. So, he's going to pay for your trip and to go to the conference for your birthday and Mom, Dad, and I are going to come with you for support and for a much-needed vacation. I'm so excited! A grown-up family vacation! What do you want to do about Frankie? Do you want him to come?"

"Oh, God no, he'll ruin it!"

I know that seems mean, but he really would. He didn't like my sister, he didn't like music, and he definitely didn't like me doing anything of my own. I wasn't going to let him come on this trip and sabotage it. I knew I would have to deal with months of pouting because of going on this trip without him, but on that day, I was too excited to care. I was going to Nashville.

Camille had done it again. Pushed me, like she pushed everyone around her into her world. And for the first time, I wasn't angry about it.

CHAPTER 12

Camilleland

Have you ever had someone cut you off in traffic? What have you thought of doing? Not what did you do, but what did you want to do? Have you been bullied in school? What revenge did you imagine taking? What did you actually do? Did you ever have a crush on someone? What did you want to do? What did you actually do? Did you ever want to get a specific job? What steps did you imagine taking? What did you actually pursue?

Have you ever wanted to travel somewhere new? What adventures did you picture? Where did you actually go? Camille lived in the land where all the scenarios most of us play out in our minds, she did.

A guy in a truck was speeding across the bridge as my mother and Camille were crossing it to come to visit me. Camille was eight months pregnant with Gabriel. The truck cut her off and nearly drove a pregnant Camille, my mother, and her son Mitchell off the bridge. She caught the guy at the next light, jumped out of the car and when he wouldn't step out of the car to face her, she grabbed a hacksaw out of the back of his truck and attempted to saw his truck in half with it until the light turned green. He tailed her to my house, and she showed up at my door with a police car behind her.

Camille was in Bolivar, TN taking courses to become a Certified Flight Instructor when she met Andy, a handsome, British flight student. She was 23 and very much still dating Sean. She called home and shocked us all, especially Sean, by announcing she would be marrying Andy. We were heartbroken for Sean, as he had been around for so many years that he was very much a part of our family. She somehow convinced me and my parents to join her in England to meet Andy's family.

My father only made it a couple days in England before he announced, "This is stupid and the weather sucks" and returned home.

Camille, my mother, and I traveled all over England with Andy as our guide. Within a month we had met Andy's family, seen every bloody castle in England, and watched Camille get bored of Andy. We returned home with some great shoes and sans Andy. Camille went back to her True North, Sean.

Sean always wanted to be a commercial pilot but had settled in with a nice career as an airline mechanic. Camille was 25 and working as a flight attendant for Delta. She had to give up on her dream of being a professional pilot because her eyes were too bad, and they had yet to perfect Lasik surgery. But in her mind, Sean had no excuse. Sean came home from work one day and she had a nice suit she had purchased him lying on the bed.

"We're going down to UPS today for you to drop off a resume! I heard they're hiring."

Sean knew Camille well enough to just go with the flow, but thought it was a futile move. No one hires like that. They pulled into the parking lot at UPS and there was a woman struggling to carry some boxes in. Sean and Camille offered to help her.

She asked what they were doing there and Camille said, "He's here to get a job."

It turned out that the woman they were helping was in Human Resources and returned the favor by placing Sean's resume on the top of the pile. Sean still works as a pilot for UPS to this day.

High school was a miserable experience for Camille. After her Puerto Rico incident, she bounced around from school to school, never finding her niche. She wasn't good with groups and wasn't into typical teenage things. It made her both an outsider and a target. By her senior year she had transferred into the last of the area schools and she was just looking to quietly graduate and get out. Of course, one girl kept bullying her and making nasty comments to her in the hallway.

Camille went to the school office and got the girl's address by lying and saying she had homework to drop off to her. She went to the girl's house and knocked on the door and her mother answered.

"Hi. I'm Camille Kennedy. Your daughter won't stop picking on me at school. I don't want to end up in a fight at school and get expelled because I have nowhere left to go. Basically, I'm here to fight your daughter."

The mother stood stunned for a moment. "You know what...okay. I told her over and over again that her mouth would get her in trouble one day!"

The girl's mother pushed her daughter out on the porch. Camille beat her up on her own front porch and then peacefully went through the rest of the school year.

I used to argue with Camille about her wanton behavior. I would say, "You don't live in a bubble, Camille! Your actions affect all of us. This isn't Camilleland!"

It would make me so angry when she would just look at me confused and say, "So?"

I started to realize then and I definitely realize now that her bubble wasn't always bad. As much as Camille lived her life without a care about her actions or their consequences on others, I lived in my mother's world of appearances. The life where it didn't matter what was good, only what *looked* good. It was never about what I *wanted* to do, it was simply about what I *should* do.

My sister would read an endless stream of self-help books and was an expert in at-home diagnosis of illnesses, in particular, mental illnesses.

It was so hilarious when she would call me and read, "...marked by compulsive behaviors, manic phases, temporary depression...who does that sound like? WHO does that sound like?"

I really wanted to say, "Ah...you," but believe me that was the wrong answer.

I would scramble to think of someone else who would fit her profile before she got mad. It always ended up applied to some poor friend or family member. Without them knowing it, they were now under her care. She was better than any psychologist I have ever known at diagnosing behavioral disorders: bipolar, sociopathic, narcissistic borderline, you name it, she knew someone who had it and she was going to fix them.

If you have ever had a family member, good friend, or maybe even a boss with bipolar disorder, you learn to know the drill. You ride the ride that is their life so many times that you memorize every twist and turn and at some point, you can feel and predict the turns before they even come. All of us who loved Camille just strapped in for the majority of our lives and held on. Her crazy became the nucleus of what we all spun around.

Welcome aboard the bipolar express.

The ride starts with a marked increase in activity; they are too happy, too busy. They bite off more projects they can chew and buzz around like the Tasmanian Devil trying to get all the errands and projects completed.

Tick. Tick.

Ticking up the top of the roller coaster you go with them. They start to get tired, sullen, and irritable. But they keep pushing the activity level and pushing their mental boundaries.

Tick. Tick.

You are teetering at the top of the ride now with your stomach in a knot – waiting for the descent. Then it happens. And "*it*" can be anything. A broken fingernail. A mistake in something they did. Maybe they forget to get milk at the store. It really doesn't matter what the *it* is. They have now snapped.

They fall without direction and oftentimes not even on who the intended person is. Whoosh. Whoosh. Down the roller coaster you go, but something is wrong. The cables have come loose and there really isn't anything you can do to stop the ride. You fall with them fast, banging up against the edges. You are helpless to stop it. All you can do is hold on and hope for the best, and assess the damage afterwards.

As the ride finally comes to a screeching halt, there is sadness, deep sadness. It was the kind of sadness that would sometimes keep Camille in bed for days. Then, after some days of rest and a brief visit to the blessed peaceful flat tracks of the ride, it would begin again.

Tick. Tick.

Sometimes during her time on the flat tracks, she would actually go seek the help of a psychiatrist. My mother has saved at her house a whole shoebox of antidepressants with all three of Camille's last names on them and years that chronicle her life. But every bottle, missing only a few pills. I asked her in what turned out to be our final days together why she never stayed on any of the medications and her answer both made me sad and also actually helped me finally understand her.

"Lana, I feel nothing on those pills. Do you understand? Nothing."

"I know, Camille, they numb you, but wouldn't it be better for you and all of us to take them and calm down a little?"

She then asked if I had ever seen the movie Steel Magnolias, which of course I had.

She quoted a line in it to me. *"I would rather live 15 minutes of wonderful than a lifetime of nothing special."*

It's funny how I had 29 years to get to know my sister but knew her better than ever in her final days. I always thought her constant diagnosing was done out of judgment and it was so irritating because she was so far from perfect. I came to realize that she was surrounding herself with the broken because she felt equally damaged and would busy herself healing them, rather than herself. I worked hard to not let anyone see my brokenness. But she knew I was broken inside and that I just worked harder to hide my cracks. Her death made me no longer willing or able to make things pretty – not even myself.

CHAPTER 13

Crazytown

With my trip to Nashville secured, my sister felt relaxed in her obsession with fixing me and started to disclose to me what was happening in her life, and in particular, her new marriage. Although Camille would often tell anyone, even complete strangers, her problems often in much more detail than they would prefer, she wouldn't always tell the whole truth. She had already told me about her new husband's ex-wife and their monster daughter who lived with them full-time. Many of the things she was telling me were not adding up and I knew Camille knew better. She was so smart about men, and she had been driven to the point of insanity by a bad guy or two, so when she constantly referred to Lee's ex-wife, Sally, as crazy, I finally had to break down and confront her.

"Camille, does somebody really get that far into Crazytown without someone driving them there and dropping them off?" I asked, trying to put a funny spin on it.

I knew how she was; if she wasn't yet ready to out Lee as the bad guy that I suspected him of being, I risked her getting extremely mad by the accusation. But by December she was ready to tell me the whole truth of what was going on in their new family, and it was so much worse than I had imagined.

I never liked Lee. Ever. I met him through my husband and my father-in-law. They had become friends while working on a construction job together. My husband and father-in-law were commercial painters and Lee, an electrician, owned Lee's Power. Lee began to hang around my in-laws' home, coming to parties for Steelers games and other family get-togethers. I wasn't the only one to dislike him. Frankie's mother and sister both got a similar vibe from him that he was a misogynist. It was just the way he would look at you when you spoke to him. There was a seething anger under his cold demeanor. He would often completely ignore you when you were speaking directly to him very clearly. Frankie and his father swore it was because he was amid a bitter divorce, but it just felt like something more than that to all of us.

Lee was a small guy, about 5'9" with brown hair and hazel eyes. In my estimation he was not a bad looking guy, just not my type. He was, however, very much my sister's type. After her divorce, she was crying about, "who will want me as a divorcee with three kids?" I could kick myself for ever mentioning his name to her.

"Camille, there are two guys around town that I know that are around your age, divorced and your type. One is Larry and the other is Lee. Larry's a great guy, so...you'll go for Lee."

It was a prophetic statement because within a month my husband invited Lee to a last-minute family brunch we were having in Pittsburgh. When he entered the restaurant, he made a beeline for my sister. He had never met her before but had heard through conversation that she was single. He pulled his chair up next to her, a complete stranger to him, and they were an item ever since. I thought it was so bizarre; this guy who would never bother answering me even if I asked him a direct question had the guts to just pull up a chair and chat up my sister in front of her whole family. I told Camille at the time how odd I found that, and she chalked it up to him not bothering with women if they were unavailable.

Lee used his divorce as an excuse for why he wasn't showing much income. He didn't want his ex-wife to get any of it. He and his daughter moved into the house that Sean had bought for Camille and the kids, and he agreed to take care of the bills, as he was now living there rent-free. When Camille and Lee got married, he insisted that *she* sign a prenuptial agreement. This was insulting to Camille. She owned a $200,000 house outright. She owned a $30,000 car outright. Both of those things were part of her divorce settlement from Sean. She also had investments in the tens of thousands of dollars and savings built up from being a flight attendant for so many years. Lee listed his assets in a prenuptial agreement, as well. He listed them in the million-dollar range. He was a millionaire by his own admission. Once they got married, the story changed.

Lee insisted to Camille that his bankruptcy was just for show; it was a way to keep his ex-wife from getting any money out of him. But Camille wasn't getting any money from him either. She began to charge groceries and her living expenses. Lee then asked her for a $30,000 loan to buy his diesel work truck. She re-financed her home to give him the money. He then told her that a balloon payment was due at the run-down warehouse that he used for his business, and he needed an additional $60,000 to pay for it or he would lose it. When Camille told me about this, $30,000 was already gone and the paperwork was in process for $60,000. It was during a phone conversation in mid-December that she came clean to me about the loans. I couldn't believe she had done something so dumb, but I was cautious of jumping all over her. I could tell she was embarrassed by her error in judgment and

I didn't want to make her feel worse. I just sat there with my mouth hanging open when she told me about giving him all this money and asked, "What are you going to do?"

As the December days passed, Camille's stories of Lee worsened.

"I'm starting to think you're right, Lana. I think he's responsible for driving his ex-wife crazy."

"Why do you say that now?"

"I don't think he has a conscience. I used to think that he was just incredibly calm. But I can be furious with him, yelling, and he'll just fall right asleep like I'm not even talking to him."

That didn't seem to be an important thing, but I knew what Camille was talking about. It was the same icy demeanor I saw in him when we first met.

"He also did something so terrible that I don't want to tell you," she whispered.

"Oh, now you have to tell me!"

"Well, you know how his dog out at the warehouse had puppies. Well, he couldn't get rid of the last one. Mitchell and Gabriel fell in love with it. I would take them out there every day to feed it. We asked if we could keep it and he said no."

"That's not that big of a deal, Camille."

"I'm not finished. We went out there the other day and the puppy was gone. I asked him what he did with it and he told me he got rid of it. He told me as plain as day that he drove down the back roads by his warehouse and threw it out the window of the moving vehicle. Lana, he was smiling when he told me." She started to cry. "He didn't even care that I was crying. He looked at me puzzled and walked away. There's something wrong with him. It's the same thing that's wrong with his daughter. It's like they're sociopaths."

I sat in horror listening to that story. I was speechless and disgusted but tried to sit as still as possible. I knew if I reacted, she would spiral.

Camille remained obsessive throughout the entire month of December. The money, Lee's evil behavior, tapes of Ashley and her mother plotting – her mind was going at a breakneck pace.

Tick. Tick.

Camille had suggested that we give out presents on Christmas Eve rather than Christmas Day. This was something we never did, but we agreed to the break in tradition. Camille happily handed out handmade blankets to everyone there. In my gift, she included three additional items. She had made scarves from the fleece left over from the blankets and embellished them with iron-ons. One scarf was a black and white pattern of musical notes embellished with a single note. The other scarf was a red plaid pattern, embellished with two intertwined hearts.

She pointed at the hearts and said, "Us."

The last gift was a book called, "*Sisters are Forever*." On the inside she wrote, "*To my sister and my best friend, Love, Camille*." Camille was always thoughtful, but this was over the top, even for her.

Camille avoided Lee the entire evening, but not in a way that was obvious. Instead, she stuck close to Sean. Although Sean was her ex-husband, they remained the best of friends. He was a part of our family, and this was non-negotiable to Camille in any other relationship. I came up the stairs from a trip down to the game room to check on the children and saw Camille sitting on the piano bench with Sean. Her head was on his shoulder, and he was petting her hair like a father would soothe a child. Camille seemed melancholy that evening, but it was by far one of the most peaceful evenings we had had in a long time.

The peace only lasted a day. My mom called me two days after Christmas and asked if I had talked to Camille yet. I hadn't.

"Well, she's furious with Lee about his stupid Christmas present."

"What did he get her?"

"A cell phone with 300 minutes. He got a phone for one of his workers and gave her the free one that came with it. She's on a rampage!"

I got off the phone with my mother and called her immediately.

Tick. Tick.

She answered the phone breathless and hostile. "Hello!"

"So…Mom told me about the phone."

She started on a non-stop tear on Lee. Here it came, the truth – full of all the swear words she could muster.

She detailed with fury and sadness the last couple of days.

"That no good motherfucker! I give him $90,000 and he gives me a *free* phone with 300 minutes?"

The 300 minutes was a particular slight because anyone who knew Camille knew that she could go through that in a day. There was never a time that you saw her without the phone to her ear. Of course, with Camille, her anger was more about everything else going on than a bad gift.

"He and his daughter take over my house. Ashley insists on taking the boys' room, the biggest bedroom in the house. I do it. She kicks Mitchell in the face and calls him names. He does nothing about it.

He doesn't help with the bills. I charge shit I need. His fucking ex-wife makes my life miserable, and he does nothing about that either. I gave him $90,000! Am I fucking insane?"

I took the opportunity when I felt she was ready to hear it. "Camille, have you given him the $60,000 yet?"

"No. It hasn't come in yet."

"Don't. You're crazy to do it. What if he leaves you with all that debt? You're remortgaging a house that's paid for. You'll have to go back to work immediately. Do you really want to do that when the kids are so young?"

"But I already told him I would do it."

"Tough shit. You must look out for yourself and the kids. You've only been married for 18 months, and you're going to give him $90,000? That's nuts, Camille. Nuts!" I was so relieved to finally say that to her. It had been eating me up since she confessed about the loans.

"What are you going to do?" I asked.

"I don't know. I don't know. I don't know. I'll call you tomorrow." She hung up.

When I hadn't heard from her by 1:00 PM the next day, I called her.

"Hello," she answered, sounding angrier than before but less frantic. I knew that sound in her voice; she was on a mission.

"The $60,000 has come in and I'm at the bank to get it before he does. He's not getting a fucking dime more of my money. I'll call you later."

Those were the last words I ever heard from my sister's mouth. Seven hours later I was in my car speeding to her house.

CHAPTER 14

A World Without Her

They were true to their word. It was hours before we were able to see Camille again. We waited in what they call a "Family Room," an oversized room that is shared with other families of patients in critical condition. They finally came and ushered us in to see her. She was now lying still on a respirator, surrounded by machines and beeping monitors. IVs sprung from her veins. I touched her leg, and she was as stiff as a piece of cement. After hours of waiting to see her, there was a feeling of *now what?* It was 3 AM and the neurologist who would care for her would not be in until later in the morning.

I finally called my husband, and he pushed for me to come home.

"There's nothing you can do there right now, Lana. You need to come home and get some sleep."

I agreed and we all left for the evening.

My parents dropped me off at my house at 4 AM. It seemed oddly unfamiliar to me. There were dishes in the sink, so I started to load the dishwasher. I wandered around straightening up the kids' toys. I went to the bathroom and ran icy water over my face. My husband finally heard me and came down the stairs.

"What are you doing?" he asked. "Go to bed. I'll stay downstairs, so you can have the bed to yourself."

I pulled off my clothes, put on my nightgown, and lay alone in bed. Visions and flashes of my sister started going off like lightning strikes in my mind. I just wanted to sleep a little. But the moment I would start to slip off, I would see her again. I started to kick my legs in frustration.

I pounded my fists on the bed and without knowing what I was really saying I started to scream, "I want my sister! I want my sister back!"

Frankie ran into the room.

"What the hell? You scared me to death! What are you doing?"

I was already up and packing an overnight bag with anything I could get my hands on.

"I'm going back to the hospital. And I am not coming back without her – one way or another."

Frankie drove me back down to the hospital without a fight. On the way down, a Phil Collins song, "Against All Odds," came on the radio. Phil Collins was a favorite for me, Camille, and my dad. We would drive up to the little airport together blasting his albums.

"How can I just let you walk away, just let you leave without a trace…but you coming back to me is against all odds…."

The words found new meaning to me, and I buried my face in my hands and cried the whole way down. I knew how this was going to end. I knew I was driving to watch her die. But I couldn't leave her alone and I wasn't the only one who felt that way. Without consultation, when I arrived at the hospital my mother and father had also returned. Sean had now joined them.

Lee was at home.

The days and hours that followed were a haze of visitors, doctors, and strangers. My mother, father, Sean, and I were the constants. Lee would come and go, which I found weird, but a bit of a relief. His sister from Florida emerged with him on the next day and she never left his side. She was a bossy and abrasive woman. It seemed like she was trying to take charge of the situation, but none of us knew her. We hardly knew Lee. We definitely didn't know his sister. We were trying to go through something that was so intensely private with an audience of strangers.

Sean and I would sit and talk to pass the hours of waiting, which is all the hospital is. And then he lost his voice. He had started with a sore throat, but from days without sleep and from sheer grief, he had completely lost his ability to speak. Lee, on the other hand, would go home each night. He claimed to be "keeping an eye on Ashley," but she was 13 and he had family to watch her. One morning he came in and walked by me. I sniffed the air. Cologne. Sean, my mother, my father, and I had not slept since the night before the incident. We had been in the same clothes for days. We may have brushed our teeth...may have. Because I was spending all this time in a germ-infested hospital, I asked my doctor to call in a prescription for antibiotics. When my husband brought it to me, he slipped in a painkiller and forgot to tell me. I unknowingly took the painkiller and started to see birds flying around the Family Room. So, here I am ducking from imaginary birds in three-day old underwear and her husband is well-rested wearing cologne. I found it so sad for her.

The question about the respirator came quickly. The neurologists were trying a few things to "reboot" her brain, but all the results showed zero brain activity from the lack of oxygen. After a few days of no activity, I went up to the cafeteria to ask my father what we should do. Oddly enough, my typically harsh and fatalistic father didn't want to admit she was gone.

"It's not really our decision to make, Lana. Technically, it is Lee's by law."

On my way back down from the cafeteria, the neurologist caught me in the hall and asked if the family had considered organ donation. He had just come from examining Camille and had tears in his eyes. My mother had placed a picture of her three kids in her hand. They were all dressed up for Halloween as characters from Monsters, Inc.

"I'm sorry," he said. "I have three children at home and a wife around her age." I was touched by his genuine emotion.

I smiled at him. "I would love for her to be an organ donor. They let you meet the people who are the recipients now, don't they?"

Just then, Lee interrupted. "She is *not* going to be an organ donor. We discussed it. She told me she didn't want to do that."

I turned and glared at him. "When did she say that? That doesn't sound like her at all. I'll tell you what…where's her purse? Get her driver's license. Let that decide!"

"Doesn't matter what her license says. I say no," Lee said and walked away.

The neurologist looked at me, disappointed. "Once again, I'm sorry."

I started to pray that no one would have to make the final decision to take her off the respirator. It is impossible to get a doctor to give you a zero percent chance of any recovery, and that was what we all wanted. I prayed that it would be an easier decision for us. The next thing I knew, they were hurriedly wheeling Camille down the hall for more tests. The doctor gathered us all into the Family Room and told us that Camille's brain had begun to uncontrollably swell and that any hope of any type of meaningful recovery was gone. Lee and my father nodded at each other and right there the decision was made to remove her from the machines that were keeping her alive.

The nurse warned us it could be hours or days before she finally passed after the removal of life support. It was days. We gathered around her bed. No one took much time being out of her room, except for Lee. Some of her friends came to visit. A kind priest, who was a friend of our family, came and administered Last Rites, even though she wasn't Catholic. Her friend Tracey stayed right through the night on New Year's Eve. We sat around her and told stories as if she were still there.

I would sometimes say things I knew she wouldn't agree with and say, "Come on, Camille. Fight with me. Stay with me. Stay with me just a little longer."

I would comb her hair and sprinkle her with dusting powder in her favorite scent from Bath and Body Works, Warm Vanilla Sugar.

Amid the pain of her final days, Lee's family would come along to make it worse. On her final day, Lee's mother arrived. I had never met her, primarily because she refused to accept my sister. She had called her a gold digger, which was so infuriating considering the true situation. She made it clear in my sister's life that she had no time for her, and I was not happy that she came there, but I am always civil. The 80-year-old woman walked into Camille's room on a cane and stood silent for a moment.

She finally turned to me and asked, "Is she an organ donor?"

"Well, I wanted her to be but no, your son is refusing…"

Before I was able to finish my sentence she interrupted me. "Darn. 'Cause my knees are shot and I could really use her bone."

My eyes widened and I turned and walked straight through the curtain into the hallway. There stood Camille's friend, Lydia. "Who are these people?" I whispered.

The nurse came in on January 2nd and told us that it wouldn't be long before she passed. After several days and much morphine, her vitals were now slipping. We all gathered around her. My father held her hand, my mother held her other hand, I sat and put my hand on her leg, Sean and Lydia sat near the end of the bed. Lee was nowhere to be found. Her final moment came quietly.

We watched the green line rise and fall with her heartbeat. The line slowed in its rise and frequency, and then it went flat. The nurse came and turned off the beeping monitors and there in the silence she drew her last breath. Deafening silence. There were days in the hospital that I just wanted it to be over with. It was clear that she was brain dead, and that the sister I knew would never be again. But there was more to having her breathing body in front of me than I knew, than we all knew. We lingered by her lifeless body in silence and finally one by one we walked through the curtain into our new world without her.

CHAPTER 15

Nobody Said It Out Loud

My mother and father quickly left the hospital. I went to the Family Room to gather my things. Lydia and Sean waited for me, leaning on the silver railings in the hallway with their heads hanging down. We met in the hallway and silently made our way out of the hospital. No one said a word. I kept looking behind me, stopping, lingering. I had the uneasy feeling you get when you leave for a trip, the feeling that you are forgetting something but magnified by 1000. I made it halfway down the hall and it dawned on me.

"How the hell did this happen?" I asked. "Why is my sister dead?"

Lydia and Sean looked at me and said, "I don't know."

I rushed back down the hall to the nurse's station.

"Where's my sister's doctor? I want to know how she died. Why is my sister dead? Get her doctor now, please."

The nurse just stared at me.

"Now! Why is my sister dead? I want to know." I raised my voice uncharacteristically.

This is the part that is so difficult for people to understand. How could it take us so long to ask that question? Lee had immediately thrown out the notion of a "*massive heart attack*" which we all thought was inaccurate and odd. But once we got to the hospital the focus shifted to her brain death and the possibility of her making any kind of meaningful recovery. Then, there was the grief and disorientation of not sleeping for days. For whatever reason, we ignored the obvious and the obvious was this; something had happened to stop her heart, to stop her from breathing and it had caused her brain to die and her body along with it. So, what was that something? An autopsy would have provided that information, but along with the organ donation, Lee had refused the autopsy.

In his words, "She came into this world whole. Let her go out whole."

My mother pleaded with him that Camille had three children and a sister and if there was some sort of undiagnosed genetic reason for all of this, we needed to know. But he continued to refuse.

The nurse got on the phone and paged my sister's doctor. Sean, Lydia, and I waited in front of the nurse's station for what seemed like forever for him to return.

Finally, he came and I asked again, "Why is my sister dead? Not the brain death, but what caused that?"

He shrugged his shoulders and looked hesitant.

"It's possible that it was viral myocarditis. It's possible that this triggered a heart arrhythmia and that stopped her heart."

"Okay. Can you spell that for me? M-y-o-c-a-r-d-i-t-i-s. Is this what I tell people? You keep saying *possible*."

"Well, it's impossible to say for sure without an autopsy."

"Well, then do one!"

"I'm sorry. You are not next of kin. I've told you too much already. Only her husband has the right to her information and to demand the autopsy. He refused one."

Next of kin, what an odd term. It is meant to indicate the closest relative to you. It doesn't go by length of time or strength of bond. This is the person who has all the power over decisions made for you in positions like these, and the minute you get married, your next of kin becomes your spouse. You better really know and trust them, and they better really know and trust you. When you say, "I do" you hand over so much more than a ring, you hand over your life in a lot of ways. So, here I was with this guy who had only been around 13 months making decisions that affected my entire family. The anger in me began to well up as we left the doctor with more questions than answers.

As we were walking, I asked, referring to Lee, "Where the hell is he, anyway? Why wasn't he there when she died?"

Lydia hung her head. "I didn't want to tell you this, but rumors are starting to swirl around town."

"What?! What are people saying?"

"Well," she said hesitantly, "One person told me they heard it was a drug overdose and another person asked me if she was anorexic."

"How dare they...where is this coming from...my God!"

Lydia shook her head. "I don't know. I know that's not true, but you know how small towns are."

The fact that within the five days that she lay dying, people in our hometown had turned her death into something that might be her fault made me sick to my stomach and even more insistent that we find the real cause of her death. Lee stood in the way of that, and me, Sean, and Lydia stood now in the cold parking garage under the hospital and wondered why.

Why would Lee refuse the autopsy? Why would Lee refuse organ donation? Why did he breeze in and out of the hospital not seeming to be grieving like the rest of us? Why did he immediately tell my father and the hospital that she had a massive heart attack? Why did he bury his head in his hands and fake cry whenever I or anyone asked him pointed questions about the evening of the incident? Why did he leave the hospital and not stay with his wife when he was told she would be dying soon? How could he have been completely dressed by the time I got to the house? He said he came out of the shower and found her, and he did CPR until the EMTs got there. Why was he completely dressed when I got there? How could two healthy people in their thirties die in the same house within six months?

The questions began swirling around the parking garage like a cold breeze. Each of us was adding our own questions to the mix and the breeze turned into a cyclone of doubt. Yet, no one wanted to say the answer out loud but then simultaneously we all said our final question: "Do you think Lee had some hand in her death? Maybe even Alan's death?"

There was a lot of "oh my Gods and me toos and I didn't want to say anythings" that followed from each of us. We stood there and talked about little things that had been bothering us for the last five days. But no one would say the word, the word that seemed so preposterous, so unheard of. No one would say it out loud because it was too insane of an accusation. No one would say it because it was too cruel if we were wrong.

No one that evening would say the word murder, not that evening, not yet.

CHAPTER 16

Semper Fidelis

Something happens to you when someone you love dies. It's like they die, but you become the ghost. I wandered disembodied through the days following my sister's death. I was floating and see-through. Funerals are so cruel. They force you to do the ordinary when everything ceases to be ordinary. Wake up, brush your teeth, wash your hair, get dressed; they seem so meaningless. I stood in the mirror pulling my long, naturally curly hair straight, and thought, *why am I doing this?* The routine of it all felt so frivolous and vain. I just wanted to go to bed, but the funeral forces you to move, to plan, to organize when all you want to do is disappear. Meeting with a funeral director, picking out flowers, and writing an obituary just seem like tricks to keep the ghosts busy. As a ghost, I passed in and out of those moments and only remember them as flashes.

My mother, father, Lee, his sister (who had no place being there) and I met with a cranky funeral director. I had no idea why the funeral director was so grumpy, and it struck me as such an odd demeanor for somebody in his profession. He took us to the basement to look at caskets like they were used cars. Lee chose the least expensive model. As much as I disliked him, I didn't mind the choice. I am a relatively practical girl, and it did seem like quite a waste to bury $5,000 in the ground. We then made our way upstairs to a round table to make decisions on the funeral, how many days, and how many viewing. When the text for the obituary came up the mundane meeting went south. Lee kept insisting that her obituary read, *Camille was survived by two sons, Gabriel and Mitchell, and two daughters, Ashley and Nicole*. This was untrue. We felt like it was a slight to Ashley's mother and asked that it read, *survived by her sons, Mitchell and Gabriel, daughter Nicole, and stepdaughter Ashley*. Why was it such a big deal to have Ashley listed as her daughter? Like everything else, his behavior made no sense at the time.

His next decision was just absurd. When we were going over her employment, 17 years as a flight attendant for Delta, he added "and president of Lee Power."

"What?" we collectively asked.

"Yeah, I made her president of my company," he replied with an arrogant tone in his voice.

We scoffed at the idea that he had truly made my sister president of his company. He was a self-employed electrician. Why in the world would she be listed as president of his company? It made no sense. Our final conflict was over him listing her cause of death as viral myocarditis. I knew from my discussion with the doctor that this was also not accurate. But my mother, father and I sat there helpless as non-next of kin and had no choice but to accept the publication of an inaccurate and bizarre obituary. My suspicion of Lee grew, and several times during this meeting I caught myself just watching him, observing. He would catch me staring at him and quickly look away. Similar to the hospital, he seemed entirely detached from my whole family, always huddled with his sister, in his own camp. But these were lines he drew. It was becoming increasingly clear that there was a division between us, and it was growing wider.

I didn't dare mention my suspicions to my parents. I felt foolish for thinking that he had a hand in her death, and I needed time to sort it out in my mind before I said anything to them. We had to make it through the funeral with him, and I had enough of my mother in me to not want to have any scenes being made. So I kept my mouth shut and my eyes on him. I felt the need to document and remember, to force myself out of my ghostly haze enough to see him. I would repeatedly watch him bury his face in his hands and cry whenever he was pushed further about details of the evening of her death. I would say in my mind, *Lana, don't look away, don't look away.* I would watch him come up with a dry face and think to myself, *No tears? You're sobbing so hard that you're moaning and without tears?* I felt he could read the doubt on my face. In the moments our eyes would connect, a cold chill would run down my spine. What I saw in his eyes was a mixture of fear and contempt. He saw me seeing through him.

Our next trip was to Camille's house to pick out an outfit for her to wear in her casket. Once again, we were treated as unwelcome visitors by Lee, his friends and family who were crowding the house. His mother, who refused to step foot in Camille's house because she was "a gold-digging, single mom" was now camped out at Camille's kitchen table. Her kitchen table was diner style, a table with a wraparound booth. My mother bought it for her. My parents bought the vast majority of the furniture in the house for Camille when she moved there. My father took one look at the crowd and opted to sit in the car. My mother and I went alone into the house. We said awkward hellos and made our way to Camille's bedroom. Camille's closet was nearly bare. My sister's closet was always neatly crowded with the finest clothes. She had exquisite taste and passionately believed in the idea of a 'complete outfit.' She would have the pants, shirt, belt, shoes, purse, and jewelry to match. But there was hardly one thing left.

"Where are all my sister's clothes?" I asked Lee, visibly annoyed.

"That's it," he said with a shrug and walked out of the room.

"It certainly is not all of her stuff!"

My mother and I kept looking at each other with raised eyebrows as we searched for her things. We settled on her Delta uniform as her final outfit because it was really the only complete outfit left in her closet. We tried to settle ourselves by saying, "Well, she really loved flying and working for Delta," but we were fuming on the inside. I went into her large free-standing cherry wood jewelry box to pick her a pair of earrings and found it in the same condition as her closet, nearly bare.

This time, I went after Lee for the answer. "Where is my sister's jewelry? Where is her stuff? All that's left is the costume pieces?"

This time he said, "Well, there's a lot of people in the house. So, I moved it out to my warehouse."

"But there's a lock on the bedroom door, Lee. Why wouldn't you just lock the door?"

As he had done so many times before, he just looked at me with no response and walked away. We picked a pair of costume pearl earrings, once again because there wasn't much else to choose from. In her jewelry box, I spotted the cross of my grandmother's that she was wearing on Christmas Eve.

"I want this," I said to my mother.

"Leave it, Lana. There will be time for all of that later."

I waved my hand toward her empty closet and jewelry box. "Really?"

I tucked the cross into my jeans when my mother turned her back.

Our next stop was to pick out flowers for the funeral. As we made our way down the main road of town, my father said he was calling Lee to find out where all her clothes had gone. My father dialed as we made our way up the hill past an elementary school. Lee didn't answer the phone and the machine picked up.

It was Camille cheerily saying, "Hi! We're not home right now. Leave your name and...."

The unexpected sound of her voice melted my father. He dropped the phone and went limp in his seat sobbing. He let go of the steering wheel and the large Chevy Tahoe was now careening down the busy road unmanned.

"Joseph! Joseph!" my mother yelped, tugging at his arm. She was so concerned with him that she seemed unaware for a moment that no one was driving the vehicle.

"Mom, you have to hit the brake!" I screamed from the back seat as I reached up over his shoulder and aimed the steering wheel to the right to avoid oncoming traffic.

We jumped the truck over a large curb leading into an auto body shop. The curb slowed us enough for my mother to grab my father's limp leg and use it to push the brake. I reached again from the back seat and threw the truck into park. We sat there in the parking lot with the engine running. My mother and I stunned silent, my father sobbing uncontrollably. After a moment, my mother exited the passenger side, went around the truck, and opened the driver's side door.

"Come on, Joseph," she said sweetly.

He got out, still sobbing, and let my mother place him in the passenger's seat and take the wheel.

My dad's brother, my uncle Mark, lived near where we were stopped. My mother drove the Tahoe to his house. My father sat hunched and sobbing in the passenger's side of the car. I fought back the tears. It was so painful to hear my father weep and to see him curled up like an injured child.

Oh, Dad, it will be okay, I thought but didn't speak.

We arrived at my uncle Mark's house and my mother got out and walked up the sidewalk to the front door. My mom went in and emerged with my uncle following behind her.

He opened the passenger door and said, "Come on, brother" and grabbed my dad's arm and wrapped it around his neck.

He pulled him from the truck and walked with my father's arm wrapped around him like a wounded soldier. I watched the two brothers, two Marines, two Vietnam Veterans, make their way down the sidewalk together, Semper Fi. I felt a twinge of self-pity. With my only sibling gone, who would stand by me when I was too weak to stand alone?

I got out of the back seat and into the driver's seat of the Tahoe. "I'll drive."

My mother was visibly shaken from the ordeal but still holding it together. I pointed the car toward the florist and filled the awkward silence with humor.

"Geez," I said, "Never send a man to do a woman's job!" My mom laughed. I continued, "It's amazing what a man will do to get out of shopping for flowers!" My mom laughed again.

Inappropriate humor is, was, and will always be my hiding place.

CHAPTER 17

It's Like I'm Brain Dead

I don't remember getting ready for Camille's funeral. I don't remember driving there, who brought me, or walking into the funeral home. Those are details I wouldn't mind remembering, they just aren't there. They say that your mind blocks out the painful memories until you are ready to deal with them, but my mind doesn't seem to work that way. I'm sure I wore black, but I couldn't tell you the details of my outfit. I think my husband probably drove me to the funeral, but I don't remember the ride. But I can remember in burning detail the moment they opened the folding doors to reveal Camille's body to the family.

My grandma was sitting in a wheelchair. She was still very much able to walk, but my mother felt that the grief would make her too unsteady on her feet. My mother, grandmother, and I went to her casket. This was the first time my grandma had seen her. My mother never took her to the hospital.

My grandma sat in the chair and cried, "My poor little baby, my poor little baby." She just kept saying it, over and over again.

My mother and I looked at Camille and simultaneously said to each other, "She looks terrible!"

Now, I know dead people aren't supposed to look good, but she looked particularly bad. Her bob-length hair was teased into a blonde helmet-looking hairdo and her makeup was all wrong. On top of that, her mouth was frozen in such a way that, for lack of better words, she looked pissed! Appropriate, I suppose, but awful nonetheless.

There was nothing we could do to change her final and awful last expression, but my mother asked me to help her fix the rest. We quickly ran and closed the bi-fold doors before others started to arrive. My mother picked at her hair and I pulled my makeup out of my purse. I drew on her cold stiff mouth with my lip liner while taking deep breaths. I knew how morbid this was. I powdered some bronzer on her face and some pink blush on her cheeks. It was only a small improvement.

"This really isn't her color," I said to my mom.

I always wore deeper tones of red and burgundy on my lips and golden shades on my eyes. Camille was always more partial to the pastels.

"It's okay, Lana. Thank you."

Putting new lipstick on my sister in her coffin brought to mind the stories my sister and I would share about our mother with us in the delivery room.

Camille was in labor with Mitchell and my mom came in and looked at her and said, "Oh, Camille, that isn't the right color lipstick for you."

"Then fix it, Mom!" Camille replied, irritated. My mom switched Camille's lipstick.

When I gave birth to Michael my face was all broken out from the pregnancy hormones. My mom came in and saw me and started to dab my neck and face with concealer.

"People will be taking pictures, you know."

"Death, girls…is no reason to look terrible," I imagined my mom saying.

I wrapped up my sister's coffin makeover just as people and flowers flooded the room. It was all too overwhelming for me. I didn't know where to stand. My mom told me I should be up near the casket, and I can vaguely recall forming a sort of receiving line. A constant stream of people began to pass by me, stopping to hug me and offer condolences. I couldn't stand any longer. Someone got me a chair and I sat during most of it. I would stand up, hug someone, nod my head and sit back down. A woman came up to my mom and hugged her. She struggled to find the right words to say.

"Oh, Marlene, I don't know what to say to you right now…it's like I'm brain-dead." The woman no sooner got the words out of her mouth than she realized what she had said. "Oh my God, I'm so sorry! I meant to say…." She gasped.

"It's okay," my mom replied.

I just started laughing which I'm sure didn't make the woman feel any better. Once I started to laugh, I couldn't stop. The hysterical laughter turned into hysterical tears.

Sean chose not to bring the children to the funeral. He didn't want that to be the last way they saw their mother. We were uncertain if that was really the right thing to do, but we didn't question his instincts on it. It was a rough call for him to make and as their father it was totally his decision. I have to wonder if, because they didn't see her at the funeral, did they have the closure they needed? Only time will tell. I know that after Alan's funeral and even though I attended it, I played a little mind game with myself that he went back to Florida. I would let myself think that he wasn't dead, he had just moved away. I wondered if her kids would do that. I wondered if deep down they would believe that she just left them because they never saw her actually…dead.

Lee was there, and busy working the room. I watched him bounce from person to person, shaking hands like he was at a class reunion. Once again, I was angered by his nonchalant attitude. We hadn't spoken to or seen one another since the awkward day before. I could see my parents starting to watch him with suspicious eyes, but we still hadn't spoken too much about him. My mother was definitely beginning to express concerns about Camille's things after we saw her empty closet and jewelry box. As before, we were split into camps. My family on one side and Lee's on the other. I didn't think other people noticed, but apparently, they did. We heard after the funeral from many friends and family members that they had left commenting on his lack of visible grief. One friend of my father's said he had to be pulled out by another friend because he was going to hit him after witnessing him joking around and laughing.

One of my mother's relatives reported that her normally unsuspicious husband left shaking his head saying, "Something just isn't right here. Something about that husband of hers just isn't right."

Something being "just not right" was the feeling that seemed to be the theme of all of the events.

There was one person at the funeral who I made a concerted effort to pull myself together enough to meet, Sammy Blackburn. Camille told me many stories about Mr. Blackburn, Lee's friend and attorney. He had overseen Lee's divorce, custody battle, bankruptcy, and pre-nuptial agreement with Camille. Camille told me that Lee had told her that he exchanged legal representation from Sammy for electrical work.

"How much freaking electrical work could one guy need?" she would ask, amazed. "Sammy will do anything for Lee. It's suspicious."

Camille did not like Sammy. She felt like in the original draft of the pre-nup that he had written it very one-sided to Lee's favor. Why she didn't initially see that Lee was the one guiding Sammy, I have no idea. She had it in her mind that Sammy was writing an unfair agreement to protect his friend. In the end, she started to see that the two of them were working together, and she felt extremely uncomfortable knowing that Lee had a "free" attorney at his disposal. I just had a gut feeling that Sammy would be coming into play with my family very soon and made a point to meet him face-to-face.

I asked someone there to point him out to me. He was sitting in a chair in a room adjoined to the viewing room having a conversation. As I made my way over to him, he saw me coming out of the corner of his eye and stood up to meet me. He was a tall imposing man in a suit that appeared cheaper than what I would expect for a lawyer.

"I'm sorry to interrupt, but I wanted to introduce myself. I'm Camille's sister, Lana," I said, shaking his hand firmly.

"Hello, Lana," he said with an uncomfortable look on his face. He made no further attempt to continue the conversation. He instead repeatedly looked down at the woman he was speaking to as if to prompt me to walk away. I stood there for a few additional moments, sensing his discomfort.

"Okay, "I said, "I just wanted to put a face to the name." I turned and walked away.

We made our way through the viewing and to the day of her burial. After the minister's final blessing in the funeral home, we gathered around Camille's body for our final look at her beautiful face before the casket closed forever. I stood near her trying to memorize her face: the fullness of her bottom lip, the way it was slightly flattened, her cheekbone, her jaw line. I wanted to see her smile again because I already couldn't remember what side her dimple was on. She had one big dimple on one of her cheeks. *Which side was it?* I thought. I think it was the left side. I stepped a few feet away from her as Lee approached, allowing him to have his last moments with his wife.

Lee looked at her for a second, then reached down and took her hand. But he wasn't holding or stroking it, he was pulling at the ring on her finger. Their engagement ring was made from a rather large canary diamond that Camille was given *prior* to her meeting Lee by one of her many suitors. The ring was on her finger in the casket. Yes, she allowed Lee to use the diamond she received from someone else to be reset and used as their engagement ring. I am sure the funeral director would have arranged to get it returned to the family. Apparently, Lee wanted to make sure he got it.

I stood in horror, watching as he yanked and pried to get the ring off her stiff hand. He finally freed the ring and turned to catch me watching him with my jaw hanging open. He put the ring in a little purple drawstring bag, slipped it in his pocket and without a word gave me a slight smirk and walked away.

The taste of vomit rose in my mouth. I looked at my sister one more time. It was the final violation of her. The tears welled in my eyes. I clenched my jaw and fists, and fought back the vomit and tears, as I peered across the funeral home to catch the back of Lee's head as he walked out. That was the first moment that I felt the warm rush of pure hatred flow through my body. My whole body was hot, then went ice cold. My hands and knees began to shake uncontrollably first, then the rest of my body. My eyes narrowed. I closed them trying to erase the image of him prying her ring off her cold, helpless hand, but it was burned there along with his telling smirk forever.

Just as I had literally felt pain in my heart as if it was physically breaking when Camille lay dying in the hospital, I felt the physical poison of hatred in my body. It made my breathing heavy, my body feel stronger, and it made me stand up straight from the slouch that the grief had created. There was a strange power in it. I left the funeral home, looking back at Camille for the final time to make my way to the church for her final blessing.

The irony of sitting in church, a place of love and forgiveness, feeling nothing but hatred and pain was not lost on me. By this point, the pleasantries between Lee's camp and ours were over. Like a wedding, we sat in the large, packed Presbyterian church split down the middle, our side on the right, his on the left. Alan's father Charlie sat next to me on my right. They played Josh Groban's "To Where You Are." I leaned my head on Charlie's shoulder and sobbed. My husband sat to my left, but I paid him no mind. At that point, I had lost all interest in phony consolation. I wanted to share my grief with people who were truly lost without her. Alan and Charlie both loved and understood Camille. I leaned into those who loved her purely.

My cousin, a local blues singer, got up and sang "Amazing Grace" a capella. I doubled over at the waist because I couldn't catch my breath during the song. Camille always felt like she was lost and flawed. Was she really found now? Was she finally free?

CHAPTER 18

Murder

In the two weeks after my sister's burial, my mother joined me, Sean, and a growing number of Camille's friends who believed there was something odd about Camille's death and that Lee may have had some hand in it. But we were all walking a fine line because there were some things of Camille's that we wanted her children to have, and Lee was now the keeper of those things. My mother had become fixated on a few items of Camille's, her wedding ring and Nicole's antique crib. These were two items that she insisted had to go to Camille's children. She made arrangements with Lee to meet at my dad's office to get the items and he never showed up, and he stopped answering phone calls.

Sean's suspicions of Lee also continued to grow. He recalled that in the days after Alan's death, Lee approached Sean to take his name off the mortgage.

"I'm just trying to look out for you, Sean," Lee told him. "Alan's ex-wife may try to sue or something because he died here. I wouldn't want that to be on you."

Lo and behold, Lee immediately had paperwork drawn up by, who else, Sammy Blackburn, and presented it to Sean unexpectedly right there at

Camille's kitchen table. Sean signed the house over to Camille's name exclusively. Sean told me later that he was uncomfortable with the decision but couldn't think of how putting the house in just Camille's name could benefit Lee. He never thought she would die six months later.

Sean was holding onto a shred of hope that Lee would do what was right. Sean felt that the home should be sold, and any profit be divided equally between Camille's children and Lee. Honestly, I thought that was too generous of an offer. Sean was able to have one phone conversation with Lee.

As I listened in, he said, "Hey, buddy, how about you bring Ashley up to Cranberry to the Burger King? The kids can play in the indoor playground there and we can discuss what will be done with Camille's things."

Lee agreed to come, but again never showed up. Instead, Sean received a letter from Sammy Blackburn stating that Sean was "no longer to contact Mr. McConnell."

Then, I received a phone call from Mr. Blackburn.

"Hello, Lana. This is Sammy Blackburn. I was calling to inform you that your sister made out a will prior to her death. All of her belongings are to go to Lee, and he has no financial responsibility to her children. Even if there wasn't a will, Pennsylvania's Surviving Spouse Law would have all her assets transferring to him anyway."

I sat stunned for a moment. "A will? She made out a will? A will that left everything to him and not her children? She would never do that! A will seven months prior to her untimely and unexpected death? How convenient, Sammy!"

"Well, Lana. It's legal and it is the way it is."

"Sammy, there's a difference between what's legal and what's ethical."

"I'm sure there is, but that doesn't change the fact that everything is Lee's and there is nothing you can do about it. Thank you. Goodbye."

I slammed down the phone and felt the hatred rise again. I looked over at the Christmas tree that I had asked my husband to repeatedly take down, still sitting in the living room. I lifted it from its base and threw it down the basement stairs and screamed. It shattered and crashed as it hit the final stair in pieces.

"I said to take it down! I don't want to see it! I don't want to see any of it!" I screamed into the air because no one but me was home.

Days later, the phone rang again. This time, it was the local police department.

"Lana, I am calling to inquire about your sister's death."

"Yes," I said anxiously.

"Two young people died in the same house within six months. Do you find that odd?"

"Yes, I find it odd! I found it odd all along!"

I started to get into the story, but they asked that I come later that day to the station to tell them of my suspicions. I got out of sweatpants and did my hair for the first time since the funeral to go to the police department. I was filled with a strange rush of excitement and fear. Until that point, the suspicions flew around our friends and family, but no one seemed to have the nerve to go to the police. My father, typically the boldest of us all, was still bedridden with grief. My mother felt like I had been the most vigilant during the whole event and that I was also more well-spoken under pressure than she was, therefore, the responsibility of the official accusation fell on me. I became the voice for us all.

I arrived at the local police station and announced my presence to the police officer manning the little reception window. The wood door next to the window opened and I was ushered through the department to a back office. It was set up like the interview rooms you see on television, a long table with two chairs. I took a seat, and the officer took the chair at the head of the table. There were two other officers standing in the room near the door. I recognized the ice-blue eyes of one of them as the officer who was on the scene the day of Alan's death and the evening of the incident at my sister's house and nodded at him.

The interviewing officer pulled out a notepad and began to ask me questions. I recounted to him the evening of the phone call. I backed up and told him about the loans, my conversation with Camille at the bank that day, the tape recording my sister made of Ashley and her mother, Lee's behavior throughout, his refusal of organ donation and autopsy, and the will that I had just found out about. The officer took notes on everything I was saying. Every once in a while, he would raise his eyebrow with a look of suspicion in his face and look back at the officers standing behind him.

I feared going there that they would think I was just a crazy, grieving sibling looking for someone to blame for her sister's tragic death. As much as I disliked Lee, as much as I was suspicious of him, this was a hard enough admission to make to myself and an even harder accusation. I needed the police to understand how deeply I wanted to believe that my sister died in any other way than murder. I needed them to prove to me that our suspicions were wrong.

I wanted to believe anything else, but the facts wouldn't allow me that peace. As I finished answering their questions, I looked up and met eyes with the officer. He had a very serious look on his face. He gave me no indication at all of any kind of disbelief, indeed it was quite the contrary. The contemplative looks in his face told me that my observations and suspicions were valid in their eyes. He told me they would be in touch, and I left.

CHAPTER 19

Bloody Marys and Fuzzy Slippers

The reality of what had just happened hit me as I drove away. They were now investigating Lee for murdering my sister.

Somehow, although that was always my suspicion, something about going through the questioning with the police made it so real. It was too much to wrap my mind around. I felt my adrenaline begin to rush through my body. I went to my husband's parents' house where he had taken the children. I was frantically explaining the questioning that I had gone through. They were shocked but looked at me with a quiet reserve. My husband's aunt walked into the house, and I began retelling the story to her. Aunt Katie was my mother-in-law's sister. She was larger than life and louder than anyone I had ever known. I was happy that she had walked in because she was at least reacting to my story.

"Holy shit, Lala! They think this guy killed your sister? Holy shit, you poor girl!"

Lala was a nickname his family gave me because of my now non-existent happy nature. I found it ironic for her to call me that at that moment.

"Let's go get a drink!" she shouted.

Katie liked to drink. She liked to drink a lot. At that moment, I really needed to blow off some steam. I asked my husband for permission, and I left to go to a nearby restaurant to have a drink with her.

Since getting married and having children, I rarely drank and my nights out were exceedingly rare. The bartender asked me what I wanted, and I couldn't think straight enough to even know what to order.

"She'll take a Bloody Mary," Aunt Katie finally answered for me.

I sat with her and recapped the events of the last few weeks. After four Bloody Marys, I was drunk. I chose, stupidly, to drive home. As the vodka hit my system, it seemed to melt the shock and disbelief into anger. This was real. It wasn't just me being suspicious. The police were suspicious, too. They were actually investigating this guy for murdering my sister.

"Murder, murder, murder," I kept hearing in my head.

I kept envisioning my sister. First, she was with me alive and laughing at the pool. Then, I would see her lying in the hospital bed. I would rub my eyes and see her in her coffin. Then I would see his face. The anger welled and my car weaved.

By the grace of God, I made it home. I came through the door and Frankie and the kids were already in bed. My cell phone rang, and it was Sean.

"Hey, how about I just drove by the scumbag in Fox Chapel?" he said.

"Really?" I slurred. "I'm gonna go get him." I grabbed a beer out of the refrigerator.

"Are you drunk?"

"Yup, pretty sure I am. The police interviewed me tonight. They think he could have killed her, maybe even Alan. I'm not sure how to process that. So, I am currently processing alcohol. Seems easier. Where did you say you saw that fucker?"

"You should get some sleep, Lana," Sean said, shifting his tone to concern.

"Nope. I'm gonna go get him," I mumbled.

Sleep was something that now eluded me. I spent so many nights living on bad coffee in the hospital, forcing myself to stay awake to be with her, that my sleep pattern was completely messed up. I had not slept for weeks at that point. The police interview mixed with alcohol had now just added an extra layer of insanity.

Frankie must have heard me and came down the stairs.

"What are you doing?" he said angrily.

"I'm gonna go get him," I slurred again, dialing the phone.

He rolled his eyes at me. I looked back at him in disgust and thought, *how dare you? Do you know how many times I have had to stare at you drunk and acting stupid over the years? At least I have a reason. At least I will admit it.*

But all I managed to spit out was, "I know I'm drunk. I'm looking for someone to drive me. He's in Fox Chapel and I'm gonna get him. You coming?"

He just stood and stared at me with his mouth hanging open a little and shaking his head no.

I fumbled my cell phone out of my purse and called my friend, Jillian.

"I'm drunk and I need you to come get me and drive me to Fox Chapel."

"Okay, I'll be right over."

"See that, Fraaaaaankie," I said, drawing his name out to taunt him. "Jillian is my friend. You're not my friend. Nope. You're barely my husband."

"Shut the fuck up, Lana and go to bed," he angrily replied.

I started clapping my hands together like I was singing a 'shut the fuck up' song.

"Shut *(clap)* the *(clap)* fuck *(clap)* up. Shut *(clap)* the *(clap)* fuck *(clap)* up. That's what all the boys say. But you can just go away."

He took one more long stare at me, turned on his heels and walked up the stairs to bed.

"Buh-bye." I waved to his back.

I saw the headlights of Jillian's car as she arrived in front of my house. She lightly beeped the horn, announcing her arrival. I grabbed a picture of me and Camille that was sitting on my piano, another beer from the refrigerator, and ran out to her car.

"Hey, bud," she said, almost laughing. "Where we going?"

I began to recount to her the details of my day. The police station, the drinking, Frankie's apathy, and the phone call from Sean.

"I want to go to Fox Chapel and find him. I also just want to get the hell out of here."

"Okay, let's go," she said as we drove off.

 I never had to explain myself to her. I never felt like I had to prove my sanity to her. She was there the night of the "incident" at Camille's house, as we began to call it. She had come to sit with Camille's children. She had come many times to visit in the hospital as Camille died. She also believed that something was not right with the whole thing, that maybe Lee was involved. So, that night she drove me to Fox Chapel without hesitation.

The residential area of Fox Chapel, for lack of a better term, is where the rich people live. Sports stars, political figures, and executives tend to populate the town. The commercial area of Fox Chapel is a series of little strip malls, filled with franchise stores and specialty shops. It was only about a 20-minute drive from my house. As you come off the highway, it spins you into the first of the rows of strip malls. I asked Jillian to pull into it. As if we were pulled there by some magical force, we immediately came upon Lee's distinctive truck with his company name and logo on the side. My stomach dropped.

"Holy shit," I said. "There he is."

Jillian pulled in right beside his truck and we both looked at each other and kind of giggled at the fact that our mission to find him was that easy.

"Now what?" she asked.

His truck was parked right in front of a bar/restaurant. All of the other stores were closed at that time, so it was clear that he was in there somewhere.

"I guess we go in," I said, looking over at her.

The lights of the strip mall shined inside Jillian's car, and I saw for the first time that she was wearing her pajamas under her winter coat. She pulled her foot up, revealing leopard print fuzzy slippers and smiled.

"All right…let's go." She stepped out into the slushy parking lot in pajamas and slippers to come into a bar in a wealthy area to be by my side.

Real friends come out in their fuzzy slippers.

The bar was in the center of the restaurant and shaped like a big U. Tables and chairs were set up on either side. People were seated at the tables, finishing a late dinner, and talking. No one except the bartender seemed to notice us coming in and we quickly took a seat at the bar. As soon as I sat down, I spotted Lee sitting across the bar. He didn't see me, and I positioned myself behind a pole where I could watch him without being in his full view. He was sitting with a couple I didn't know to his right and a group of women stood near him to his left. He was laughing, joking, and even flirting with them. I tapped Jillian on the leg and motioned to her where he was.

"Wow," she said. "He's really grief-stricken."

I just sat there and watched him carry on like a single man out at the bar and it sickened me. Just then, the bartender broke my gaze by standing right in front of me and waving his hand.

"Hello," he said.

I broke my stare at Lee and looked up at him. He was a good-looking guy around my age.

"Well, good evening, ladies. What can I get for you?" he asked with a smile.

"Bloody Mary," I answered.

"Water," Jillian replied.

He came back over with drinks and a deck of cards. "Pick a card," he said to me.

I looked at him unamused.

"Come on." He winked. "Pick a card."

The alcohol had given me a boldness that I usually didn't have in these kinds of situations.

"Please stop trying to flirt with me. I am not in the mood," I said politely.

"Yes, please stop," Jillian chimed in.

Instead of backing off, he was intrigued. "You look like a girl on a mission. What's your story?"

I pulled the picture of me and my sister out of my coat pocket and laid it on the bar.

"This is my sister. This was his wife." I nodded my head in Lee's direction.

"Who, Lee?" the bartender said in a way that indicated he didn't like him.

"You know him?" I asked.

"No, he just showed up here hitting on all the women a week or two ago. Something about him annoys me. He seems to think he's more suave than he actually is...But the ladies seem to like him." He waved his hand towards the three women that surrounded Lee across the bar.

"Really! My sister just died two weeks ago!" I said, tapping at the picture.

"Oh, gross! What a dick!"

"You're telling me he was here days after his wife died trying to pick up women?"

Jillian asked, "Or was he in here drinking away the blues? Grieving, you know?"

"Absolutely not," he replied. "He did not look like a grieving man to me at all. Does he look like one to you?"

We all looked again at the group laughing and conversing like any normal night at a bar. Just then, Lee looked across the bar and spotted me. I didn't know what else to do but to point my finger at him. His eyes got as large as saucers, and he stood up and grabbed his coat off the back of the chair.

I stood up too and yelled out, "I want to talk to you."

But it was too late. He headed to the back of the bar, to the bathrooms, and away from the front door. I followed him to the back and then turned around to the group he was with. I wasn't going to chase him into the men's room. I was positioned so there was no way he could make it out the front door without going past me.

"So, how long have you ladies known Lee?" I said angrily.

The group of women looked at me stunned and scared.

"We just met him," they said in unison.

It quickly dawned on me what this looked like to them. It looked like I was a jealous wife or girlfriend catching him out cheating at the bar. I tried to explain, but the alcohol got in the way. I was stumbling over my words too much and I was shaking from the confrontation.

"No, no. Don't be scared of me. I'm not mad at you. I just want to ask you some questions."

One girl made eye contact with me and almost whispered, "He was talking primarily to her." She tilted her head in the direction of a blonde woman in a fur vest.

"You know he was married to my sister and she just died two weeks ago. Now, he is out hitting on you," I said to the pretty blonde woman who looked to be affluent and in her mid-forties.

She couldn't have looked more uncomfortable, and I started to get extremely embarrassed at the spectacle I was making.

"I just met him. I don't want any trouble," she said, looking at me as if I was pathetic.

I couldn't blame her. I felt pathetic.

"Okay. I just thought you should know."

I walked back over to Jillian who was watching from across the bar.

"Come on. Let's just go wait by his truck outside. I'm embarrassed now."

She agreed and we walked outside to see his truck was gone. He must have slipped out the back door and ran around the building, got his truck, and took off.

Jillian looked at me. "Why would he run? That's just so shady."

"It sure is, Jillian."

Jillian once again walked with her fuzzy slippers through the slush and jumped into her car and unlocked the door for me.

"Okay, bud. Where to next?"

She didn't seem the slightest bit rattled by the events. By this time, the buzz of the alcohol had turned to a sickening pain in my stomach.

"Just take me home."

"That's probably a good idea." She pointed the car toward home.

CHAPTER 20

Swim or Die

Mitchell, Gabriel, and Nicole came to stay with me after Camille died. Mitchell and Gabriel were enrolled in the neighboring school district to mine and Sean really wanted them to finish out the year there. We all agreed it was a good idea for them to not have to face any more changes. Sean lived in Beaver Falls, a good hour away. Plus, his house was a lovely ranch home but not equipped to have three children occupying it full-time. The house was sufficient for the weekend schedule prior to Camille's death, but he wanted to add a second floor to equip it with the additional bedrooms and bathrooms needed to raise three children full-time.

My house was now full with five small children: a seven-year-old, two five-year-olds, and two two-year-olds. It was chaotic on a daily basis. I became not much more than a short order cook. They were all particular eaters and had completely different eating habits.

"I want cereal. I want eggs. I want a snack."

It felt like all I did was cook and clean up, cook and clean up. In addition, the napping schedule that I adhered to with my children so strictly was now thrown out the window. I can recall attempting at first to clean up the toys they would drag out, but quickly gave up and only stuck to the rule that they keep them all down in the basement game room. Quickly, every toy box and snap container I had used to organize their toys was emptied all over the floor of the basement. Any sense of organization that I had in my life was gone. I had lost control of the house, the children and myself, but I was still too numb to care.

One day at my house, I heard a blistering scream from Nicole. As a mother, you get to know the difference between cries. There are the 'you took my toy cries' and there are the 'I am in terrible pain' cries. This was the latter. I ran to see the source of her pain. I found her sitting on the stairs pointing her finger at a confused Aaron. Aaron, quite in-nocently, had decided to put on Nicole's little Dora the Explorer tennis shoes and wear them around when she began to scream uncontrollably.

I leaned down to her and asked, "Nicole, why are you crying so hard? What's the big deal?"

"My shoes, my shoes," she sputtered out through her tears.

"Okay. I'll make him take them off," I answered, still confused by her dramatic reaction to tennis shoes.

"No. NOW! My mom bought me those. My mom bought me those. Take them off NOW!" she shrieked and then broke down into a deep sob.

I ran over to a still confused Aaron and quickly pulled them off his feet and handed them to her. She clung to the shoes and cried. I cradled her in my arms and rocked her. I understood now. These children were forced from the only home they had known because Lee had taken it. He held onto all of Camille's material possessions without remorse. He refused to even speak to my family to pass any of her things along to her children. Now, a two-year-old motherless little girl clung to a pair of Dora the Explorer tennis shoes for dear life, the only connection she had left to her mother. I wish all of the people who said, "They are just things" could have been there to see that moment. Then they can tell me that my sister's belongings were just things and then they could say that to her children.

The local police had turned Camille's case over to the Westmoreland County district attorney's office. The lead investigator was Detective Hughes. I remember the first time Det. Hughes called me. I had to go sit in my car in the garage to be able to hear him through all of the noise the kids were making. He was attempting to contact Lee to call him in for an interview, but he couldn't find him. When he finally did find him, they had set an appointment to meet at the police station for questioning, but Lee never showed up. He was calling me to see if I had heard from him or would have any idea where he might be. Of course, this just deepened my suspicions. It turns out that Lee had left the state and was in California, allegedly visiting friends. I kept asking if they were going to search the house, but the detective was rather tight-lipped about any further details. I would have quite a few conversations with Detective Hughes over the next few weeks and grew to like and trust him. I could hear it in his voice that he cared about our situation and the general well-being of our family and Camille's children.

The days melted into one another throughout the month of February, caring for the children, talking with the police, caring for the children more, and hanging out with Sean. One afternoon, the new normal routine of my day was broken by a call from my friend and former boss, Brian Solomon. I had been the package model and salesperson for his company that sold a variety of different gel products. They also held the trademark for the Turbie Twist hair towel. He had been talking with me for months about being the on-air spokesmodel for Turbie

Twist once QVC picked the product up, but in all the chaos, I had forgotten about the offer.

"Hey, Lana. QVC wants you, but they want to see some tape first. The Shopping Channel in Toronto is going to present some of our gel products. If you make the trip with me, I can put you on air selling a gel pad…and it's good money."

I worked for Brian and the company he represented, Pittsburgh Manufacturing, Inc., on and off throughout the years. Frankie always came between me and my professional successes. When I worked on-site for the company, he would call and call for me, to the point where it would get me in trouble.

I told Frankie about the unexpected opportunity, and I was, of course, met with irritation and resistance. I, for the first time, looked right through him and went about making plans for my television debut.

I went into my closet to start trying on outfits that might be television-worthy. I pulled on a pair of black dress pants and realized I could pull them off without even unbuttoning them. I tried on a black ribbed turtleneck, and it just hung on me. I stood naked in front of the full-length mirror on my closet door and realized how different my body looked. It was the first time in quite a while that I had gotten out of sweatpants. I hadn't even realized that I had lost so much weight. I had struggled with my weight in my early teens. I managed, even after children, to settle into a healthy size 6. Even at a 6, I always felt like a giant next to Camille's petite size 0. I examined my body in genuine shock. You could see my ribs. I looked at my legs and my usually plump thighs had shrunk to the size of my calves.

"Holy fuck. I look like Camille."

We would travel on the first day and spend the next two days doing shows. I would have a 15-minute show every two and half hours. Brian promised that on our first night up there, he would sit and review with me the selling points of the gel pad I would be presenting. I explained the details of the trip to a pouting Frankie and kissed the kids good-bye. Aaron began to whimper a little as I made my way to the door. A sulking husband and a crying child could have been enough for me to cancel just a few months prior. But I had begun to change inside. I saw it as a manipulation, at least from my husband. We needed the money, and this was a unique opportunity for me. Most of all, I really needed to get away.

I began to feel ill on the ride up to Toronto and by the time we arrived at The Shopping Channel's studio the following morning, I was in the midst of the full-blown flu. I weaved through the hallways that were packed with boxes, wires, and props. Every once in a while, we would pass a set with a host, co-host, and cameraman. It was hard for me to believe that within an hour I would be standing up there doing that. As promised, Brian had met with me the night before and reviewed the bullet points about the gel mat I would be selling and there weren't that many.

I waited in the Green Room, which was not much more than an over-sized closet with more unopened boxes and a mirror with movie star lighting. The kind of lighting that makes anyone look good. I sat and primped in the mirror and sipped on some hot tea that Brian had run to get me in the little kitchen they had set up for guest hosts. He had his eye on picking up an attractive, blonde producer and would pop his head in every few minutes to check on me and update me on his progress with the woman. He amused me with his constant pursuit of women.

As I looked at myself closely in the mirror, I couldn't believe how different I looked. The last few months had aged me. My first two wrinkles appeared in the space between my brows. My eyes looked different, sadder, older. The weight loss had made my cheekbones more pronounced than they had ever been. I was days away from my 30th birthday and it seemed that almost overnight…I looked it! I had always had such a girl-next-door look: blonde hair, blue eyes, and freckles longer than a grown woman should have them.

I leaned into the mirror and furrowed my brow to really get a close look at the battle wounds between my eyes and toasted my new reflection with my tea. "Death to Lala."

"You're up!" a crew man with a headset called to me, leaning his head through the door.

Brian came breezing in behind him. I stood up and blindly followed them to the set. A counter-height table and a chair, a cameraman and a middle-aged brunette awaited my arrival. Sitting on the table was the 18"x18" gel pad I was to be selling and an index card with the bullet points Brian had given me. The crew man who beckoned me approached me and spun me around. He clipped the battery to the back of my skirt and then spun me back around and handed me the tiny mic. I grabbed it and just stared at him. He could tell I was clueless and subtly motioned to me that I was to slide it under my shirt and clip it onto my lapel. I smiled at him and followed his direction.

He winked and said, "Believe in the product and yourself and you'll do great" and walked across the set and took his place next to the cameraman.

Below the cameraman were two television sets with a large electronic timer set to 15 minutes. I could see myself in the television set but knew instinctively not to look. I should look right into the camera. As I positioned myself to look at the camera the red light went on, the timer started its countdown and the host began to talk.

"Good morning, everyone…we are here with Lana…" the host chirped.

As she announced my presence and gave a quick briefing of the gel mat, I realized quite terrifyingly that she was using the same bullet points that Brian had given me. It was my turn to talk, and she had said everything I knew to say.

I said, "You're so right, it does do this, it does do that, and so on and so forth." I went through all of the bullet points again, looking at the host, picking the mat up and showing it to the camera. I thought I was doing pretty well. I was a natural! Then, I glanced down at the ticking timer and realized that only one minute had passed! A chill of panic went through my body.

All I could think was, "Swim or die, Lana. Swim or die!"

My father taught me to swim at six years old. He took me to Mellwood Pool. It was a huge pool and with an attached skating rink, and it was the place to be as a kid. It was the Redneck Country Club. Lots of boys swimming in cut-off jean shorts and an arcade where you could play air hockey soaking wet and intermittently electrocute yourself. I loved it there.

On the day I learned to swim, my dad, sister, and I entered the gates to Mellwood Pool. Camille, looking perfect in a bikini, broke away and found an empty spot in the grass to soak up the sun. My dad immediately took me to the water. I do recall him doing the whole, "Here sweetie, float on your belly thing" with me a few times. I shrieked and cried and that was enough for him.

He took me to the deep end, threw me in and yelled, "Swim or die, Lana."

He jumped into the pool with me but always stayed at arm's length. I would frantically doggy paddle to him. I could nearly reach him and then he would push off and swim further away. "Swim or die, Lana."

I swam the entire length of the pool that day just chasing my father. I learned that day that the desire to survive makes you learn new things fast.

The clock above the television monitors was ticking down slower than any timer I had ever seen in my life. No matter how long I seemed to talk, it felt like the seemingly endless stretch between me and my father. But by the end of the show, when I watched the final seconds tick by, I felt the same rush of fearless accomplishment I felt at Mellwood Pool. The spot ended and I took my microphone off as the adrenaline of the moment carried me back to the Green Room in a haze.

Brian walked in behind me and excitedly proclaimed, "You were fantastic!"

I turned to him like a little girl discovering a new trick, and patted my hands together. "Again. Again!"

The doggy paddling of my first shows turned into fluid strokes as the shows passed throughout the day. Unfortunately, the slight sickness I felt before heading to Toronto was turning into a full-blown flu. I could feel my cheeks getting warm from my increasing fever and my throat getting increasingly sore. In the two hours I had in between shows, I would go to my dressing room and lie on the couch. Brian would come and go, hitting on women in the studio and returning with tea for me. Twelve hours later, I was finally done. I was excited to get back to the hotel room and wash my stage makeup off and crash. The next round of shows began early the next morning and I would only be left with a few hours' sleep. I quickly packed up my things and left with Brian.

We got to Brian's vehicle and he quickly picked up his cell phone to check his missed calls and messages. I didn't bother to check my phone and opted to slouch in exhaustion in my seat. We had not even made it out of the parking lot before I could see Brian reacting in shock to his messages.

"Oh my God, Lana! You have to hear this."

He handed me the phone and I listened to at least 14 messages from my husband.

They started in a nice tone with an undercurrent of irritation. "Hey, Brian…Frankie here. Lana's not answering her phone. So, I called you. If you see her, could you have her call me?"

They ended with a screaming and maniacal Frankie, "Brian…you motherfucker! You better bring my fucking wife back…NOW!"

I was mortified. I then checked my phone and got the same progression.

"Hey, Lana…give me a call." Then, "You fucking whore…your kid is sick…I know you don't care…whore."

Then, the worst message I have ever heard. "Hi Mommy, where are you? Daddy wanted me to call. I'm sick."

139

It was Michael. His voice was hoarse from a sore throat like mine. He apparently had come down with the same flu.

The elation I had felt from accomplishing something new was gone. I sat in the car as Brian drove and lectured me.

"He's nuts. You have to get rid of this guy. The nerve of him to threaten me!"

As Brian talked, our phones began to ring again, one call after another.

"I have to answer it, Brian."

"I wouldn't."

I waited until I got back into my room and got undressed and washed off my face to answer Frankie's call.

"Hello," I said quietly.

He didn't wait to immediately start tearing into me. "I've been calling your phone all fucking day and you were not answering! What the fuck is going on?"

He was hollering so loud that my hoarse throat couldn't compete. I just sat on the bed and waited for him to stop. Some of the things he was saying were so disgusting that I just set the phone down on the bed and listened and waited until I could hear his muffled voice cease.

When I heard a pause, I picked up the phone and said, "They don't allow cell phones in the studio, you jerk! I didn't know that. I had no way to tell you."

I tried to explain that I was also getting sick and took the time between shows to rest, but he wouldn't hear me. I heard over the phone the dinging of a car door opening and the door shutting.

"I'm coming up there to get you. You better pack your shit." He slammed down the phone.

I called Brian in his room and told him the continuation of the story.

"You have to do a half day of shows tomorrow!" he proclaimed.

I was sicker now than ever. My husband had my five-year-old child call me and ask me where I was and now was possibly driving to Canada to drag me home like some Neanderthal.

But I replied, "Oh, I'm doing the shows. He's not ruining this for me. I won't allow it anymore."

This is not my life. Not anymore.

CHAPTER 21

Take the Bridge

Frankie ignored me for a few days after I returned from Toronto. He never asked how it went. I really wanted to brag a little about the accomplishment of surviving live television and how cool it was, but I knew better and chose to just avoid the topic. By this point in time, I had settled into the realization that he was never going to let me achieve anything in my life; he was too threatened by it. This was a fear that kept me back from many different opportunities, but I had changed, and he knew it. We traveled around the house silently, speaking to one another only if it pertained to the children. I took a permanent residence on the couch every night. I preferred the silence to the screaming, but I was well aware that this was just the calm before the storm.

"I'm sorry to just call you and tell you this out of the blue...um...I could get in trouble for this," said the voice on the phone.

 It was a week after my return from Toronto and I had answered the phone after dinner.

"Okay?" I said confused and curious.

"Well, are you under a rent-to-own agreement with a woman named Jenny Vento?"

"Yes. I am."

"Well, she hasn't been paying the mortgage, and your house is going to be foreclosed on. I am a mortgage broker she is working with. She's actually trying to refinance the house she's living in now and when I started to go through the process with her, I found this out. I shouldn't be telling you, but you really should know."

I shrunk down to the kitchen floor with the phone still to my ear and just stared. The kids came up to me. "Mommy...mommy...are you okay?" But I couldn't answer. "Daddy, something is wrong with Mommy."

He came walking into the kitchen and asked with irritation, "What now?"

I sat frozen. The only words I could muster were, "Gone. It's all gone now."

"What's gone?" he replied with increased anger.

"The house." I began to cry. "It's all gone now."

"Dammit, Lana, pull it together, you're scaring the children."

I tried to mutter to him about the situation we were in with the house, but I am not sure how much sense it made.

All I can remember is Frankie saying to me, "You know...you have to get over Camille's death...she's dead, you're not."

That sent me over the edge to a place I never thought I could go.

I curled up in a ball on the kitchen floor and sobbed. I kept mumbling over and over again, "It's gone. They're gone. Everything is gone. It's all gone."

I could feel Frankie standing above me watching my complete breakdown. I could hear his breathing getting heavier in anger.

Suddenly, I felt a sharp kick to my back. "Get up. Stop it."

I curled up further into the fetal position. I had completely cracked.

I felt his foot again hit me in the kidneys. "Get up now! You're scaring the kids!"

The memory of a snap of a belt rang in my ears.

The rage of a voiceless child grew inside of me as the second kick to my back hit.

Camille's voice whispered, "Get up, Lana. Get up."

I rose.

"How dare you tell me to get over it!" I screamed, stretching out of the fetal position and getting to my knees. "I haven't even got *on* it yet!" I straightened onto my feet. "I see something on television that I think is funny and I still pick up the phone to call her. I still think I see her pass me in a car on the street and wave, just to realize I just waved at a stranger. You have no idea what I am going through! Here…here…let me show you." I still had the phone in my hand. "Briiing…briiing…" I made the phone fake ring. "Here Frankie, the phone's for you…Jeffrey (his best friend) is dead. Briiing…briing…here Frankie, the phone is for you, your sister is dead. Here Frankie, the phone's for you, the house is gone. It's gone! It's all gone! Every time I pick up the phone. Gone! Gone! Gone! It's all gone!"

"You're fucking nuts, Lana! I'm calling your dad."

I grabbed the kitchen table and started banging it up and down.

"I am NOT crazy!!! I am sad. I am so sad. I have lost everything, and you kick me, literally kick me, while I am down!"

He wasn't listening to me at all anymore. I could hear him on the phone summoning my father to come.

"Lana is really losing it over here. You need to come over. I'm really worried."

"Worried? Worried?" I yelled. "You kick me in the back and tell me to get over it and then say you're worried? You're an asshole."

He turned to me and pointed toward the door. "You know, Lana…the bridge is that way. If you miss your sister so fucking bad…go be with her!"

I stood for a moment and stared at him, contemplating his offer. I went to the hall closet, grabbed my shoes and coat, and went to my car. He didn't even try to stop me as I grabbed my car keys and walked out the door. I drove my car down the road towards the Tarentum Bridge. I looked around the dark streets of the town I lived in, the area I had grown up in and it all looked blank to me. It was a small town, but it never felt as small to me as it did that evening. It felt like the town had shrunk three sizes overnight. I got to the little gas station at the start of the bridge. I pulled my car into the far end of its parking lot facing the bridge and stopped my car.

I sat with my car running and looked across the bridge. Only for a moment did I contemplate getting out of my car, walking to the edge of the bridge, and jumping. After that moment passed, another thought kept me there staring across the bridge for an hour. That thought was, *drive away.* I wondered what would happen if I just started driving. What if I just drove across that bridge, out of this damn town and away from all of this? I thought about the contents of my purse, some cash, my debit card, and a few credit cards. I could buy some clothes. I could get pretty far on the credit cards. I could just drive as far as the road would take me. I could be free.

Then, I thought of my children. I looked at Aaron's car seat perched in the back seat. I looked at Michael's toy truck that lay next to it. I thought about Mitchell, Gabriel and Nicole coming through my front door the next morning to find out I was gone. I couldn't do it. I couldn't leave them.

I tried to rationalize it. *I'm no good to them like this anyway. I could leave for a while and get my head straight. Then, come back to them. But they would never forgive me.*

The road ahead of me at home seemed so much longer and more un-known than the concept of driving off into nowhere, but I knew I had to face it. I couldn't leave my children or her children. I couldn't leave my parents to grieve alone, and I couldn't just take off and let Lee get away with what he was doing. Despair made me drive to the bridge that night, but duty turned me around.

My father was waiting with Frankie for me when I returned. I could see the relief in my father's face when I walked through the door, but behind him Frankie stood scowling. My dad reached out and hugged me. While I was still embracing my father, I replied to Frankie's scowl, "Sorry to disappoint you. I won't be joining Camille just yet!"

My father looked defeated.

"Lana, Frankie called me because he was worried about you. He thought you might do something to harm yourself."

"Really? Is that what he told you? Did he tell you he told me to go jump off the bridge! Don't let him fool you, Dad."

My dad looked at me with exhaustion and reached out his hand. In it was a tiny, yellow pill.

"Take this, honey. Please, take it. You need to sleep; we all need to sleep."

"Valium," I thought. "You're drugging me. *You* are drugging me."

I think I remember my father caving and giving me an antibiotic once as a child. Once. We took vitamins, not drugs. It was so uncharacteristic of him. *Treat the problem, not the symptom*, was a huge mantra in the chiropractic world and I had been raised on it.

I don't need a good fucking pill! I need a good fucking husband, I thought angrily.

I looked deep into my father's face and his eyes looked so tired, not just because it was nearing 1:00 AM, he looked tired deep down into his soul. I took the tiny pill from his hand and pushed it down the back of my throat and opened my mouth and stuck my tongue out like a little kid to show him it was all gone.

I hugged him and whispered, "I'm okay, Dad. I'm okay. Go home."

My father retrieved his coat from the kitchen and quickly left. I asked Frankie if we could talk. I sat him down in the unlit formal living room. He sat alone on the white couch looking out the large window that faced the street into the darkness. The only light that lit the room was the moon coming through the window. I sat halfway across the room on the floor for a few moments staring into the same darkness that Frankie looked into. It was 1:00 AM and the children were fast asleep. I needed to talk to him when they weren't around, especially considering what I was going to say.

"Frankie," I said with a deliberate calm, "I need you to look at me."

He slowly turned his gaze in my direction. "What?" he said, mimicking my calm.

"This marriage is over. I want, no…I need out," I said as he leaned forward on the couch and rested his elbows on his knees. The moonlight hit his face. "I need to ask you not to fight me on this, to just accept it. I also really need you to promise me that you won't use the kids against me…you won't try to take them from me. I couldn't bear it. I'm too tired to fight. I just want out."

He looked me dead in the eyes and kind of smiled. "I *will* use the kids against you, and I *will* fight you with everything I have if you try to go."

I could feel my hands and feet start to go numb and tingle as the Valium began to take its effect.

I looked at him as if the moon on his face lit up what he was inside. "You look like a monster, you talk like a monster, you act like a monster, but monsters don't scare me anymore."

He leaned across the coffee table and said through clenched teeth, "They should."

"Why?" I replied, whispering from the Valium. "They can't kill what's already dead."

CHAPTER 22

Grand Theft Rabbit

March proved to be a trying month. Days after the bridge incident, I got a late-night call from Sally, Lee's ex-wife. I had been putting the word out that I was trying to get in contact with her and that if anyone knew where she was to have her contact me. I knew through Camille that she was living in Ocean City, Maryland somewhere, but that she would make frequent trips back to Pennsylvania and stay with friends and family. I wanted to speak to her about Lee and see if she had any idea where he was and also if she had any insight into the situation.

The Westmoreland County detective, Detective Hughes, was in regular contact with me and was telling me that they were having a challenging time finding Lee. He had apparently returned from his impromptu trip to California, but he still wasn't answering their calls to come in and speak with them. I knew through Camille that Sally would keep in constant contact with Ashley via email and I was hoping to get his whereabouts from that connection.

"Hello, is this Lana? Camille's sister," Sally asked with the raspy voice of a chain smoker.

"Yes, it is," I replied, intuitively knowing it was Sally.

I had heard endlessly about her from Camille and seen pictures. I felt like I knew her from that but realized that I was a complete stranger to her. "Is this Sally?" I asked, already knowing the answer.

"Yeah…hey, man…I'm really sorry about your sister. I know she and I didn't get along so well, but I never would wish anything like this…" She trailed off.

"It's okay, Sally. I've been trying to find you to see if you know where Lee is. Have you spoken to Ashley? Do you know where he is?"

"Yes, I've spoken to Ashley and she is totally freaked out! You have to help me get her out of there. She's wearing her clothes, ya know. Her pajamas. Gross, right?" As she spoke, I noticed that her words were slurring as if she were inebriated in some way.

"Sally. I have no idea what you are talking about."

"Oh, man, you don't know? You don't know?" she said, raising her voice. "He's already got another girl living there and she's wearing Camille's stuff and shit. Crazy, man, right? And…you know…I wasn't your sister's biggest fan, but yuck, and I know what your family's thinking about him."

Following Sally's conversation was like trying to trace the steps of a staggering drunk. She would go from one topic to the next and I would try to rein her in.

"Wait. He has a woman living there?" Camille at that moment had only been gone for two and a half months. The revelation sent me reeling.

"Yes! Yes! That's what I'm trying to tell you. It's some blonde chick named Jennifer. Ashley's all freaked out."

I couldn't help thinking, *I don't give a shit about how Ashley feels. My family has a tape of the two of you plotting against my sister and Ashley threatening to stab Camille in the face.* But I didn't speak a word of that. I was trying to get as much information from Sally as I could, so I bit my tongue and tried to be nice to her.

"Well, that must be just horrible for her. When did this woman move in?" I pushed through her fog of thoughts trying to get answers that made sense.

"I don't know. Maybe a couple weeks ago and she's wearing her pajamas and shit. Nasty. Ashley says she woke up screamin' the other night saying she saw Camille's ghost starin' at her in the hallway. I say, good for her, wearing her clothes and shit. That just isn't right."

My stomach was tightening in a knot. I had bought Camille gorgeous pajamas for Christmas, her last Christmas. All I could envision was this other woman wearing them. I wanted to scream out loud.

I kept trying to hold it together. "Sally, the police are trying to get in touch with Lee."

"Yeah, yeah. I know what your family thinks he's done. But you gotta understand, man...my daughter's living there. My daughter..." She began to cry.

"Why are you crying, Sally?" I feigned compassion.

"I don't know what to think. I was married to the man. You know, we had these neighbors once that ticked him off and he poisoned their lawn...killed all their grass. He did it as calmly as could be. He snuck out in the middle of the night and poisoned their whole lawn. Don't know what kind of shit he put on there, but the damn grass never grew back either." Chills went up and down my spine and I sat silent, not wanting to interrupt her rant. "Then all I wanted was some time to get back on my feet and him and that damn Sammy took my kid." It seemed that now she was in a conversation with herself. "But I warned Camille. I told her he was no good. But NO! I was the bad guy. I was the bitch. I was the psycho. So, I told her and *she* wouldn't listen 'cause *he* loved *her* so much more than me. Who loves who now, Camille? Huh? How much does he love you with some other chick wearing your shit with your body still warm? Huh?"

I couldn't bite my tongue for another minute.

"Sally, Sally," I said firmly, interrupting her weird conversation between herself and my late sister. "Let's get one thing perfectly straight. It seems that you and I have a common enemy in Lee, but please do not confuse that with us being friends. You did as much as you could to make my sister's last year of life as miserable as possible, a fact I will not forget. I want to know where Lee is so that the police are able to question him and I want *any* information you may have or get in regard to my sister's death, but, and it is a big BUT, do not EVER disrespect my sister to me!"

There was silence on the other end of the phone for a moment. "Okay. Sorry. It's just that I warned her..." she began again.

"Sally, enough!"

"Well, okay. You know, I could keep talking to Ashley and tell you what I found out. But I gotta get my kid out of there. What I was thinking is maybe your dad could help me with an attorney. See, Lee has good, old Sammy to do all his legal stuff for free and I'm tapped out. Maybe your dad could get me some money, you know, to get Ashley back and then maybe she can tell us some more stuff."

A shakedown! She wants money, I thought.

"Sally, that isn't going to happen," I responded in disgust. The conversation ended quickly after that.

I was left to sit on the fact that Lee had a new woman living in the house until the rest of the world woke up the next morning. It was nearing the end of March, and I sat on the couch and listened to the sweet sounds of the birds chirping in the spring weather, as I waited for the sun to come up to start making my calls. In my mind, I had made a major discovery. Lee very well could have been cheating on Camille, I thought. How else could he get so close with a woman that she would move in within two months?

We had been able to obtain a copy of Camille's pre-nuptial agreement and there was a provision in there for cheating. In simple terms, it stated that if one or the other spouse was caught cheating that they would lose everything. In my mind, I had a motive. What had happened that night? Had Camille found out about Jennifer? If she had, Lee knew he would lose everything. What would he do to not lose everything?

We were also able to obtain a copy of some weird will that my sister supposedly signed, that none of us knew existed and guess who the witness was…Alan! Alan hated Lee, and he witnessed a will that signed all of Camille's assets over to him? Never. But gee, can't ask him if or why he would do that because he was dead, too.

I called Detective Hughes to tell him about my weird phone call from Sally; the grass poisoning, the 'I warned your sisters,' and especially the woman now living in the house and wearing her clothes.

"Yeah, wow, Lana. He's a real scumbag. But you know scumbag doesn't equal murderer," he said with a tone that I knew would have been accompanied by a pat on the head if we were talking in person.

I tried extremely hard to shake off the condescending tone and not get angry. "Yes. I am aware of that. I am also certain that ALL murderers are scumbags. So, I'm not sure how that math works out. "

"Ha," he laughed and said, "Touché. Hey, I can also tell you that he will be coming in next week for an interview. It took some time because he switched attorneys. He is now represented by Mr. Blackburn's brother. He's a criminal defense attorney. They'll be coming in on Tuesday."

"So, let me get this straight. All you asked him was to speak to him about my sister's death and he leaves town and dodges you for months. He says he's coming in and doesn't show. Now, he's coming with a criminal defense attorney. That's not bizarre to you?"

All I wanted was some validation, but I didn't get any. I have found that lawyers and law enforcement officials are very well-trained to stay neutral and to avoid any rush to judgments. Hughes was *really* good at that, and it annoyed me.

I called my mother and got the amount of shock from my news that I craved.

"What?! He has another woman living there? What?"

I filled her in on all of the details of my conversation with Sally. At this point, my mother's suspicions of Lee went as deep if not deeper than mine. Once she received copies of both the ridiculous new will and the prenup, she was busy going from attorney to attorney to see if there was anything that could be legally salvaged for Camille's children. She would spend $250/hour to hear repeatedly, "By law it is all his, even without the will. He was the surviving spouse." My father was starting to get angered by her expenditures for justice.

"Marlene, there's nothing you can do," he would yell at her. "I don't want to go broke trying. It's futile."

It wasn't as much about the things for my mother. She is such a moral woman that she simply believed that right was right, no matter what the law says and that surely someone would have to agree to that. Those inaccurate thoughts, quite frankly, kept her going like a wind-up toy banging into the same wall without the good sense to stop or turn. It was painful to watch.

"But Sean bought the house, her car, her jewelry for her. We bought the furniture and artwork. It should go to her kids, not him," she would say.

You would explain to her that it was awful but legal. She'd spend another $250 for another attorney to tell her it was awful but legal.

Then she would look at you with puppy dog eyes and go, "But Sean bought the house, her car, her jewelry. We bought her furniture and artwork."

She was stuck on repeat, trapped in grief and injustice.

I didn't know what else to do with the knowledge that Lee had moved a new woman into my sister's house who was wearing her clothes. To be honest, nobody but my mother and I really seemed to care. My dad was at the point where he could hear no more, Frankie wasn't speaking to me, and it infuriated Sean too deeply. I kind of felt like a boxer jumping back and forth in his corner before the beginning of a fight or in between rounds; staying warm, staying loose, except I didn't have a damn soul to fight, and it was making me anxious.

Just then my mom called me right as I was picking Michael up from morning kindergarten and said, "Well, I drove by Camille's house on my way to pick up Gabriel from preschool. I couldn't stop myself from driving by. There was an Easter Bunny outside. I bought her that at

Target last year. I guess this other woman is already decorating her house."

That was it for me, ding ding! I turned my car towards Lower Burrell.

It was a lovely day in late March, it was definitely going out like a lamb. It was one of those first really warm days in spring, the kind that gets everybody outside working in the yard or walking. So, when I pulled up in front of Camille's house at noon, it wasn't a surprise to see that there were neighbors out tending to their lawns.

"Kids," I said, looking at Michael and Aaron both strapped into car seats in the back, "Stealing is bad. This isn't stealing. This is retrieving."

They just looked at me confused. I marched out of the car and grabbed the six-foot, painted metal rabbit from the front lawn and carried it to my car. I quickly realized it was going to be too tall to fit in my Jeep Liberty without laying the seats down, which was impossible because the kids were in the car, so I came up with another idea. I opened the sunroof of my Jeep, popped the rabbit in between my kids with its head sticking out of the sunroof, shut the doors and drove off. The neighbors just kind of sat there and stared at me in amazement. There I was, driving through my old neighborhood with a giant rabbit head sticking out of my sunroof. This is not my life!

I didn't make it a mile before my phone rang.

"Hello."

"Lana, this is Detective Hughes." He spoke slowly. "What are you doing?" He said it in such a way that I knew he knew exactly what I was doing.

"I'm taking the rabbit back," I said, fully realizing how stupid it sounded. "I can't believe he called the cops! He possibly murdered my sister, and it has taken you guys two and a half months to find him. I take a rabbit and you find me in two minutes. What are you going to charge me with? Grand Theft Rabbit? You tell him that if he puts anything of my sister's outside that house, I don't care if it's a beach towel, if I can retrieve it for my sister's kids, I'm taking it!" *(There's one of those sentences again.)*

"Lana," he said slowly again, "you know, we are in the middle of a murder investigation and this doesn't help. You can't keep going off half-cocked!"

Half-cocked wasn't my style, it was Camille's.

Yet, I replied, as I drove down the road with the metal rabbit head smiling at the passing cars, "Oh...but I can."

CHAPTER 23

The March for Food

After Camille returned from Puerto Rico, she transferred into Saint Joseph High School for a while. The Catholic school made an annual trip to Washington D.C. to participate in the March for Life. Camille wanted to go and somehow, I was permitted to join the group traveling there. At barely 13, I can actually remember thinking that I was way too young to jump in on the Pro-Life/Pro-Choice debate, but the idea of getting to go to the Capitol and with high school kids, no less, really excited me. I don't think Camille's intentions were much different than mine. We got there and marched in the frigid cold for a minute before Camille proclaimed she was hungry.

"Come on. I want something decent to eat. There's got to be a restaurant nearby." She coaxed me and her reluctant schoolmate to follow her off the path of protestors.

There wasn't an open restaurant anywhere to be found, but we kept walking.

"What do we do now, Camille? We really should get back and join the group," her friend and I coaxed.

Camille was now obsessed with finding us somewhere nice to eat and ignored our requests to return. She looked at the sky as an airplane went over our heads in a clear descent.

"There!" she proclaimed. "That airplane is landing. Airplanes land in airports and airports always have restaurants nearby. We will follow the planes."

This string of logic made strange sense to me at 13. So, with Camille at the lead like a bloodhound looking up, we began our March for Food. We walked and walked and followed and followed. We crossed a bridge that felt like it was 20 miles long. Camille's friends started to shoot me *stop her* eyes and I shot *I can't* eyes back. My feet were becoming numb and sore, but no one dared complain.

Finally, Camille stopped and pointed at a lovely little restaurant nestled on the side of the road. "There!"

I was so relieved. We made our way into the warmth of the restaurant and were immediately seated.

A server with a Southern drawl came to take our order. "What brings you girls to Virginia?"

"No. We're not in Virginia. We're in Washington D.C. for the March for Life," my sister's friend replied. "We just walked here."

The waitress looked in disbelief and horror. "Girls! Goodness, you are in Virginia. You walked?!? You came across that bridge? That long, long bridge?" She bent over laughing and pointing in the direction of the bridge. "You walked clean into a different state!"

Her laughter was contagious, and we all joined in. As we sat there and ate, we all began to get concerned about how we were going to get back to the march. We were too tired to walk back, and we were also running out of time. Camille asked the waitress to call us a cab and she agreed. The foreign cab driver pulled up to the front of the restaurant and we all happily jumped in. The cab driver looked a little confused and angered to have three young teenage girls as customers. He made my sister flash her cash to him to prove we could afford the fare.

"Okay," he said in poor English after seeing the cash. "Where you go?"

"March for Life," Camille replied.

"I no know that. What street that?" he replied with increased irritation.

"No. It's not a street. It's a thing."

"I no know that."

"It's like a ton of people marching, you can't miss it. Marching…for… Life…." she repeated as if saying it slower would help him understand.

He turned and narrowed his dark eyes at her. "I no know that!"

Camille narrowed her eyes back at him and sat up straight in the back seat almost staring him down.

"LOTS OF PEOPLE," she yelled and then pulled her hands in to pantomime someone holding a sign. "DON'T KILL BABIES, DON'T KILL BABIES."

"Ohhh,. Don't kill babies. I know that."

He took off driving like a bat out of hell, easily the scariest cab ride I have ever had. We all just sat stunned still and held onto one another in the back seat. He zoomed in and out of traffic nearly hitting a few people and then would lay on his horn and flap his hands at the pedestrian he nearly killed as if to say it was their fault.

All I could do was begin to nervously laugh, which spread to Camille and then to her friend. When, to avoid sitting in traffic, he went up on two wheels on the sidewalk and two on the road, my laughter turned to hysterics. "We're gonna die. We're gonna die at the March for Life," I said with tears of laughter running down my face.

He finally came to a screeching halt and pointed to the mass of marchers. "Dere you go. Don't Kill Babies! Now you pay."

My sister quickly handed him the money and we jumped out of the cab happy to be alive. The march was actually now at the very end and we folded ourselves back into the crowd. We knew the number of the bus we had to find amidst the mass of school and charter buses. We quickly found ours and stepped on. No one even noticed we were gone for the whole march, and we giggled about our secret trip to Virginia the whole way home.

CHAPTER 24

Nashville Virgin

Camille had forced me into the trip to Nashville to attend the Nashville Songwriters Association International conference before she died. Technically, she forced my dad to pay for it. When the itinerary and trip details started hitting my inbox, I wasn't sure why I would even still go. But considering that at that time I was stealing giant rabbits out of Lee's yard, and had five children under the age of seven in my home, I wanted to get away.

The airport in Nashville was bright and sunny upon our arrival. My father couldn't come on the trip we had all planned to take together because he had missed so much work after Camille's death, so my mother and I traveled alone. Just walking through the foreign airport gave me a rush. All I could think to myself was, *none of these people know me. It's so great. None of them know me.* Going places around my town had become so difficult for me. Whether it was real or perceived, I always felt watched in my hometown. Did I look too happy? Were people going to judge me for laughing too soon after my sister had died? Did I look too sad? Was I making people feel uncomfortable? Is that woman over there giving me a dirty look? Maybe she is related to Lee? Does she hate me? It was like the walls were closing in around me. I walked through the automatic doors into the southern spring air and inhaled deeply and for the first time in months, I breathed again.

I wondered if this was how Camille felt when she first fled to Puerto Rico – this momentary release from being who everyone expected you to be. The difference was, she'd run away from something painful. I was running toward something I hoped might heal me. My sister's death had left a hole that seemed impossible to fill, but maybe music could help me find my way again – music that had once been my one true thing of my own before marriage and motherhood consumed me.

White shuttle buses and taxi cabs lined the sidewalk outside the airport. Country music was playing on loudspeakers and happy travelers made their way to their designated buses. We were staying at the Holiday Inn on Broadway where the Nashville Songwriters Association International Convention was being held. It was a modest, seven-story hotel that sat at the top of a hill only 4/10th of a mile from the main drag, where all the bars and action were.

Because there were initially supposed to be four of us, we had two rooms reserved. My mother and I made our way across the crowded lobby to the front desk to check in. The hotel was full of the same energy as the airport. It seemed like everybody was happy and it was contagious. The girl at the check-in desk was pretty and cheerful.

"Are you with the NSAI Convention?"

I nodded and she checked the computer for our reservations. "This says there are supposed to be four of you. Are you missing some people?"

"We are," I replied, aware of the double meaning in my reply. "It will be just us."

She smiled and continued checking us in. I was given the key for Room 625. My mother was given Room 630, just down the hall.

I could see the signs for the convention already going up on display boards throughout the lobby. "Welcome NSAI!" There was a sign that read, "NSAI Convention" with an arrow and I followed it, dragging my bags behind me. My mother followed. A short hallway led to a large convention room with double doors that were propped open. I peeked my head into the room to see several workers setting up. There were hundreds of chairs facing a stage at the front of the room. The workers were currently setting up two six-foot tables on the stage and skirting them. I had a sense of relief seeing the room being put together and knowing that the convention was the real thing. Even though Diane Warren's assistant had recommended the convention to me, I was a bit leery. There was a part of me that worried that the convention was going to consist of me and four crazy ladies who wanted to be songwriters.

We made our way to the elevators and up to the top floor to our rooms. It was about 3:00 PM and we made plans to rest a little, freshen up, and go walk around to find a place to eat. I set my bags just inside the door and lay back on the bed for a moment enjoying the silence. My house had been nothing but noise since Camille had died. It was so peaceful to just lie there and hear nothing. Just then, I heard pounding, then drilling, then something that sounded like a jackhammer. I sat up and it stopped. I lay down and it started again.

What the fuck? I thought.

I picked up the hotel phone to ring my mother's room. "What's all the racket?"

She told me she had called the front desk and they told her they were doing renovations on the floor above.

"Well," I replied, "So much for resting. Do you want to just go walk around and find a place to eat?"

We had no idea exactly where we were in Nashville, but the idea of just walking and seeing where the road would take me was the spirit of adventure that I had somehow lost and had now been returned to me. I was happy to see it again. There is nothing quite like the feeling of having nothing left to lose. It is as freeing as it is saddening.

We headed out of the hotel and out into the streets of Nashville. It seemed that all of the traffic was moving down Broadway, so we followed it.

"They all seem to know where they are going...let's follow."

Now, I was the bloodhound of Broadway St. We walked downhill from the hotel and after only about a ¼ mile the street flattened out to a row of bars and restaurants. They were little and narrow, and they sat side-by-side lining the whole left side of the street. There was music coming from each one of them. As the sounds combined on the sidewalk, it seemed like one song. It sounded like the streets were singing and it was magical to me. It was so much warmer in Nashville than it was at home that it felt like I had been given an early spring. As I walked in the new warmth and in rhythm to the music of the street, I felt something I hadn't for what seemed like forever. Happy. I was so consumed by my own feelings for a while that I completely forgot about my mother quietly trailing me.

"I'm sorry, Mom. You're hungry. Let's go in somewhere," I said, breaking my stride.

We chose the next restaurant we passed and ate. My mother offered to stay out as long as I wanted to explore, but I opted to return to the hotel to try to turn in early because the next day was certain to be long.

It turned out that the insomnia I had at home followed me to Nashville. I kept myself busy in the hotel room trying to pass the time. I tried on the outfit I had chosen for the next day: black pants with turquoise paisley embroidery around the waistband, a black short sleeve shirt that had a similar pattern around the rather low-cut neckline. It looked good. I pulled out all of my toiletries and put them in their proper place in the bathroom. I did sit-ups. I looked out the window. I did more sit-ups. I changed into my pajamas and turned on the television. The Bridges of Madison County had just begun. I had read the book many years before and remember thinking that everyone said it was this great love story and I thought it glorified infidelity. I decided to watch it anyway to try to lull myself to sleep. Instead of falling asleep, I found myself engrossed in the movie. In particular, the scene where while in the car with her husband, Francesca grasped the inside of the car door for a moment, as if to open it, when she sees Robert Kincaid's truck leaving town.

"Just go! Get out of the truck you dummy," I actually said out loud in frustration. When she took her hand off the door handle, I cried. I identified with her longing.

I only got an hour of sleep, but I was strangely energized for the next morning. It was like the nervous excitement one feels on their first day of a new job. I got ready and went to my mother's room to let her know I was going to the convention for the day and that I would try to stop by and see her when I had breaks.

I waited for the elevator to make its way up to the 6th floor with a short, curly-haired man wearing gray jeans and cowboy boots. We stepped on and I pushed the button to the ground floor. The elevator opened on the 5th floor and three more people stepped on. The gentleman and I moved toward the back to give them room. The elevator stopped on the 4th floor and a Hispanic family of four with a wheeled cart holding their bags squirmed and squeezed their way onto the elevator. The curly-haired guy and I kind of looked at each other and snickered at the awkwardness of us being sandwiched so close together.

When the elevator opened on the 3rd floor to reveal 10 people and five suitcases stuffed in the elevator like it was some kind of dare, the curly-haired man called out to the elderly man standing there, "Sir, I am from the Nashville Department of Elevator Safety. We are running a test to see how many people can fit on an elevator before we plummet to our death. Please step on."

The old man looked so confused but actually stepped on. The comical stranger looked at me and we both laughed the rest of the trip down.

We all piled off the elevator and I turned the corner to the room that was holding the convention. The curly-haired man was just ahead of me.

He turned and saw me walking behind him and said jokingly, "Stop following me. Geez, first you get all up in my business on the elevator and now you're willing to sit through a songwriting convention to be near me. Have you no shame?"

"I'm not following you, sir. I actually am from the Nashville Department of Elevator Safety, and I am going to have to take you into custody for impersonating an officer," I replied very seriously.

He smiled at me. "Hi. I'm Rick." Rick appeared to be in his early fifties and had one of those faces like Bill Murray, you couldn't look at him and not laugh. He had a silly and outgoing personality that really put me at ease. The convention started with an informal continental breakfast and networking session. Rick and I stood talking as I downed about four cups of coffee.

Rick really liked to talk and did most of it that morning. By the end of the ½ hour networking session I knew he was a married insurance salesman from Los Angeles, CA. He was in a band "many moons ago" that opened for the Eagles. After the band broke up, he was a stand-up comedian. He was in Nashville to meet up with his former bandmate, Howard, who was now playing keyboards for a young singer/song-writer, Joshua, in Seattle, WA. Rick only still dabbled with songwriting but used the convention as reunion time with his old friend. It was a whirlwind of information, but it was all fascinating to me.

The convention was about to start, and Rick called his friend Howard from his cell phone. "Where you at, man? This thing's starting." He paused to listen. "Okay, okay. We'll save you a seat." He paused to listen again. "'We' is referring to me and my new best friend. You've been replaced, buddy."

He laughed and hung up and we took seats near the back. I sat on the aisle seat, Rick sat next to me, and we placed our notebooks on the two seats next to Rick to save them for Howard and Joshua.

Just as the head of the NSAI began to welcome everybody and ask everyone to be seated, Howard and Joshua came walking through the doors. Rick spotted them and started waving his arms. They quickly made their way through the crowded room. I had learned from Rick already that Howard was a high school principal by day and a musi-cian by night. Howard was about 6'3" with salt and pepper wavy hair, mostly salt, and piercing blue eyes. He was wearing a suit jacket but trying to dress it down with jeans and, of course, cowboy boots. The outfit looked way too young for his 50 plus years, but you could tell that Howard was probably a real ladies' man in his day.

Trailing right behind Howard was Joshua. He was wearing old blue jeans, a plain T-shirt, and a John Deere hat; very unassuming consider-ing the sea of big hats and boots I was now swimming in. He was also tall, just an inch or so shorter than Howard, but appeared to be no more than 25 years old. He had a boyish charm about him and sweet brown eyes. He walked with his hands in his pockets, looking down, but peeking up from under his hat with a little crooked grin on his face.

Rick put his arm around me as we stood to allow Howard and Joshua into the spots we had saved for them. "Old best friend, meet new best friend."

Howard laughed and shook my hand. "Nice trade, Rick."

Joshua smiled a little at me, but didn't shake my hand as he passed by me. The convention was already beginning and we all sat there together listening to various panelists and lecturers. Of course, Rick would add funny comments to all of us. I know how that can be annoying to some people, but he was funny enough to pull it off and his wisecracks actually helped to pass the time when the speaker got dull.

During the breaks, Joshua began to finally speak. As I listened to Joshua talk about his music, I felt a momentary pang of awareness. Back home, Camille's children were learning to navigate their world without her, and here I was, states away, connecting with strangers. I pictured Mitchell's serious face as he'd asked me if his mom was going to be okay, and the promise I'd made that I couldn't keep. The guilt mingled with something else – a sense that in these brief hours away from the weight of grief, I was finding small pieces of myself again. Perhaps that wasn't betrayal but survival.

The day was broken up into lectures and breaks. Me, Rick, Howard, and Joshua never separated. Howard became much more vocal as the day passed and he and Rick would banter back and forth on things. It was a lot of fun to listen to the reminiscences of old friends. I really love quick-witted banter, and I am actually rather good at it. It was my favorite thing to do with Camille and Alan, and I missed it. I started to jump in on it with Rick and Howard once I felt more comfortable with them and it made me "cool" in their words. Joshua stayed pretty quiet throughout the day. He was clearly amused by all that was going on, but seemed to be sitting back and observing, more than participating. Every once in a while, I would catch him looking at me and he would look away.

I tried ridiculously hard to avoid the topic, but I eventually got asked the question that I still dread to this day.

Do you have any siblings?

Just like that, the fantasy was over a little.

"When did she die?" Joshua asked.

It was the first direct question he had asked me all day.

"Almost three months ago."

I quickly explained how I found my way to Nashville and that my sister was actually supposed to be there with me and that this was my first time there. I watched them collectively make a boo-boo face at me.

"Please don't do that. Please don't give me the boo-boo face."

"Oh, I'm not giving you the boo-boo face because your sister died," Rick proclaimed. "I'm giving you the boo-boo face because you are 30 and have never been to Nashville before! You're a Nashville virgin. How sad for you."

CHAPTER 25

The Bridges of Broadway

It was the end of the first day of the NSAI convention and the guys asked if I wanted to join them for dinner. They had a car rented and were going to go to the "best steak place in Nashville." I told them my mother was with me, and I couldn't leave her behind.

Rick said, "Well bring Mama, too."

"You're silly. She won't go."

They kind of replied in unison, "Well, let's go ask her."

I felt so bad for my poor mother. I cannot imagine what she thought when I showed up at her room with three men. They were actually so silly and persuasive that my mother agreed to join us.

I got my mother alone for a moment. "They're perfectly normal and safe. I spent the entire day hanging with them."

She actually didn't seem to mind too much. I think she was simply happy to get out of her room.

We all piled into the rented SUV. Howard drove and Joshua sat up in front. Rick, my mother and I got in the back seat. We drove to the restaurant, chatting and joking around. I watched Howard from the back seat as he fiddled around pulling a CD out of the center console and putting it on. During a break in the conversation, I heard the music playing and it was great.

"Hey, turn that up," I asked. I had told the guys earlier that I wasn't really an enthusiastic fan of country music. "See, now that I like."

"That's him." He motioned to Joshua.

"Really?" replied me, my mom and Rick at the same time. "Wow."

We all got quiet as Howard turned it up further for us to listen. Rick drummed at the back of Joshua's seat.

"Damn boy! You can sing!" he called out as he reached up from behind Joshua and shook his arms.

Joshua looked back embarrassed. He really was an amazing singer; a soft alto that could smoothly rise into a falsetto in a way that sounded effortless. It was impressive and surprising. I guess I was aware that all of us were musicians of some sort, thus being there, but it never dawned on me that they would be good, let alone great.

Howard started filling the whole back seat in on Joshua and his talent.

"Oh yeah. This guy's a big deal back home."

"I am not."

"Now I see why you came out of retirement," Rick said to Howard. "You found a voice for your songs."

"Sure, but he can write, too." Howard flipped through the songs pointing out which ones were his, which were Joshua's, and which were co-writes.

They were all good, but when you really listened there was maturity to Howard's writing that Joshua had not yet achieved. Plus, Howard's songs had a lot of piano in them which of course I preferred.

"That's why he got a recording contract. He's great." Howard bragged like a father.

"I *had* a recording contract," Joshua once again corrected.

"Yeah, until Kat…" Howard said with irritation.

"Stop!" Joshua ordered. "Don't go there."

I had no idea what they were talking about, but I could tell that the conversation was taking a bad turn and was glad that our arrival at the restaurant broke the tension.

Dinner went very much like that day. There was much joking around and banter. A few drinks with dinner made everything even funnier. My mother even seemed to be enjoying herself and it was nice to see her laugh again.

After dinner, the guys said there was an open mic night at the Flying Saucer, a bar within walking distance of our hotel. We all decided to end the night there and have a few more drinks, so that we could just walk back to the hotel. My mother was a little reluctant but agreed to join us for a little bit.

We made our way into the bar and found seats right up front of the small stage. First up was a portly bald guy with overalls on. He looked like he had walked right off the farm. Then he started to fiddle around on his guitar.

He spoke into the microphone and said with a little grin, "I like this one that I wrote, primarily because it still pays my mortgage." Then he started the song that was immediately a familiar favorite to me.

Jessie is a friend / yeah, I know he's been a good friend of mine / But lately something's changed / that ain't hard to define / Jessie got himself a girl / and I want to make her mine." My mouth dropped open.

"Rick Springfield. I loved him!" I yelled over the music.

Joshua was sitting next to me and started to smile and we both started singing the chorus along with him.

And she's watching him with those eyes / And she's loving him with that body / I just know it…Oh I wish that I had Jessie's girl…

This caught the attention of the songwriter on stage and when he hit the chorus the next time he said, "Back up, please" and motioned for us to join in again. Our whole group joined in to sing along.

"My wife's name is Kat," Joshua said out of the blue.

"Okay. I heard you and Howard in the car talking about her. Is there a problem there? I noticed you got tense when her name was brought up," I asked without thinking whether or not that was inappropriate to ask.

Joshua leaned in. "Howard hates her. He thinks she's purposely holding me back. It's my fault as much as hers." He stopped. "I shouldn't be telling you this. Forget it."

The next performer took the stage. She was a plus-sized woman with a beautiful face, brown hair, and a wide, pretty smile accented by deep dimples. She simply sat on a chair with her guitar and began to sing. She sat alone on the stage, but on the chorus of the song I could have sworn that she had back-up singers harmonizing with her. I twisted in my chair to look around the room for hidden singers. As I spun, I saw Joshua looking equally amazed.

"Is it just me, or is she harmonizing with herself? Is that even physically possible?" I leaned into Joshua and whispered.

"I've heard Tibetan Monks can do it," he whispered back.

"You think she's a monk?" I asked with a laugh. "That is the most amazing thing I have ever heard."

Joshua nodded in agreement, and we sat and listened in awe.

As I sat and listened to the unknown woman harmonize with herself and thought of Joshua's immense but uncompensated talent, one thought kept going through my head.

You are not good enough.

It was not insecurity speaking, it was a freeing reality. The streets of Nashville were clean, yet littered with talent that I could never compete with. But I loved it. I cherished that everyone from the server to the stranger walking past me had a dream – a gift to create something beautiful out of nothing but an instrument, their voice, and the words in between. I wasn't good enough to make a living as a songwriter, but I had found my people. My dad was right, they call them starving artists for a reason. But he was also so wrong, because those starving artists filled a hunger in me.

My mother opted out after the second singer and walked back to the hotel. Rick and Howard then huddled together continuing to reminisce about their past, which left me and Joshua to chat. In between singers taking the stage and drinks, we began to share a lot about our lives.

It turned out he wasn't 25 and had also just turned 30 in March, just like me. The one major similarity that we seemed to quickly zone in on was our marriages. We had both married young, in fact the same year and only a month apart. We both had bigger plans for our lives that we believed our spouses did not support. Both of our spouses were controlling and had over-involved parents.

"Oh, I have you beat," Joshua proclaimed. "My in-laws came on my honeymoon with us."

"No way!" I shouted back. "So did mine! I thought I was the only person in the world that had that happen."

He confessed that Howard's contention with her was that he had a record deal, but Kat was jealous of a woman who worked at the label for what he claims was for no reason. She called and basically gave the woman the "stay away from my man" speech and yelled at her. The woman was actually the record label owner's daughter, and they dropped Joshua from the label. I told him about Frankie's nutty behavior when I was in Toronto. The four of us closed the bar down and by the time I made it back to my room there was barely time to sleep. I rested for a couple hours and showered and got ready with anticipation for my next day.

The next two days were a blur of similar activity: the four of us palling around at the convention, a dinner marked by laughter and traveling to Nashville hot spot after hot spot at night. Tin Pan South, just an enormous party of singers and songwriters, was going on our last night there. Kid Rock was in one bar. Garth Brooks was in another. They would jump up on stage and jam with whomever was up there at the time. We capped off the evening at a big party on 12th and Porter. A famous country singer was walking out as the four of us were going in.

Joshua said to me, "Oh, I opened for him when he was in Seattle."

He reached out and they shook hands and then the singer looked right at me and as I passed grabbed my behind.

"He just grabbed my ass!" I said, shocked and annoyed.

Joshua heard me, looked angry, and turned as if he was going to go after him, but Howard intervened, putting his hands up to Joshua's chest.

"What are you doing, man?" Howard scolded, putting his hands on Joshua's shoulders.

Their eyes connected as they stood face to face for a moment. Howard asked the question as if it had a double meaning and we all knew what that was.

There was an attraction between Joshua and me that was immediate, palpable, and intense. We would circumnavigate our inappropriate urge to always be around the other by staying out as late as possible each night with Rick and Howard as our unknowing bodyguards. If they were there, then there was nothing wrong with it. We didn't discuss the attraction. We didn't need to. But I think there was a shared feeling that the convention would end, and we would go our separate ways. No harm. No foul.

At the end of the final evening, we all exchanged hugs and demos with our contact information with one another and made a promise that we would all meet up again next year for the next convention. Joshua hugged me last and tightest.

I returned to my room, buzzed from the evening's alcohol and the long hug from Joshua. I washed the makeup off my face and had just finished changing into sweats when I heard a light tap on the hotel room door. I opened to see Joshua, leaning up against the door frame with his guitar strapped around him, hanging from his back, and two mini bottles of vodka from the minibar.

"Nightcap?" He grinned, holding the bottles up higher.

I covered my face. "Oh my God, I look terrible," I gasped, pulling at my sweatpants, embarrassed to reveal my true self.

"What do you mean? You look perfect."

I waved my hand to invite him into the room. I didn't ask why he was there. I knew. Neither of us were wanting our time together to end.

"I see you brought your best friend with you," I said, motioning to his guitar.

"I thought maybe we could write something?"

"My piano isn't as easy to strap to my back." I laughed.

He sat on the bed and flipped his guitar around and began strumming at it.

"You don't need your piano. You own the words. Everything you've said to me this weekend sounds like a song."

"Oh!" I sat on the bed next to him. "My friend's dead, my sister's dead, my marriage is dead. All I need is a dead dog and I'm a walking country song."

He stopped strumming the guitar and looked me straight in the eyes. "No. You're perfect." He reached over to brush my hair out of my eyes.

I hung my head down. "I am not perfect. I am pain, walking, breathing, laughing pain."

"When do you hurt?" He lifted my chin up to force me to look at him.

"Only when I breathe." A single tear rolled down my face.

He moved his face within an inch of mine and neither of us could break the stare.

I put up my hand to his chest and could feel his heart rapidly beating. I slowly pushed him back, but just a little.

"Don't do anything you're going to regret," I whispered as I pushed him back a bit farther.

"That's what I'm trying to do." He moved my hand from his chest and pulled me into him.

In that kiss, for the first time in months, I felt no pain.

The next morning, I rushed to throw my clothes in my suitcase to meet my mother in the lobby to begin our trip home. I headed to the airport on the hotel shuttle bus. I missed my children so bad; this was the longest that I had ever been away from them. But everything else I was facing there made me want to kiss my mother goodbye at the airport and never get back on the plane home. I closed my eyes and envisioned doing that. Each step I took toward the gate, I lost a little more strength, and I felt like the air was leaving my lungs.

"Are you all right?" my mother asked.

"Oh, yes. I'm just really tired. I'm going to run into the bathroom and splash some cold water on my face."

I went into the airport bathroom, wet my hands, and patted my face, then turned into one of the bathroom stalls and closed the door. I leaned against the door, holding onto the cold metal coat hook for balance, and started to cry. I felt like I was given a glimpse of the life I could have had, and it was too hard to bear. What if I had just moved here at 18 and not gone to college? What would my life look like? Where would I be? Would I be a songwriter by profession? Happy with my job? Married to a guy like Joshua? Would my sister still be alive? Would Alan?

I was struck by the thought that in a lengthy list of directions, all it takes is one wrong turn to get you completely lost. Somewhere along the way, I turned left instead of right and ended up in the wrong place. This wasn't my life. This wasn't how things were supposed to be. What was my wrong turn? Could I have prevented all of this by making different decisions? If I had truly followed my dreams instead of doing what Dad told me to do, I would have never met Frankie. Therefore, Camille would never have met Lee. Alan would never have been at the house that day because there would be no house, no pool. All our lives would have been, could have been, and should have been different. It was all my fault. My God, it was all my fault.

I splashed water on my face in the bathroom again and tried to ignore that I still smelled Joshua's cologne on them. I pulled makeup from my bag, powering my face, dabbing concealer under my eyes, to hide the tears of guilt. I faked a smile in the mirror to make sure it looked real and then emerged to my waiting mother.

"Are you all right?" she repeated.

"Yes, I'm perfect."

CHAPTER 26

No Justice

The moment I came back from my Nashville escape, Frankie met me at the door.

"Did you sell a song? Can I stop working now because you're making so much money?"

"Of course not, Frankie. That's not how it works. There are so many talented people down there…"

I stopped talking because it was clear he wasn't listening anyway. He didn't care. He just wanted me home. Michael and Aaron ran and hugged me once they spotted me coming up the stairs. I dropped my bags and hugged them back. I recalled my questions and doubts at the airport and thought, but then I wouldn't have them. I wouldn't have my boys.

"Was it fun, Mommy?" Michael asked.

"Yes, it was, Michael. It was really fun."

"Cool." He started to pull my arm toward the kitchen.

Aaron still clung to my leg. "Look what I drew."

I rubbed his soft blonde hair and scooped Aaron up onto my hip as I looked at his picture of a tank drawn with incredible detail for a five-year-old. Just like that, life was back to normal.

Sean returned with the three other children the next day and I was so grateful to have him there to listen to all the details of my trip. He was very encouraging and understanding of the feelings that I had. It seemed like he had picked up right where Camille had left off; supportive of my efforts to follow my own path in life and to get out from under Frankie's thumb. He listened and then filled me in on the police finally getting Lee in for an interview. He confessed to sitting in his car in the late March snow outside of the police station to watch Lee walk in.

"You know, I thought I would feel some justice or gratification watching him walk in. But the S.O.B. pulled up to the police station in his black Mercedes and got out with his attorney, Blackburn's brother! Can you believe it…Blackburn's brother is a criminal defense attorney? And he just left the car running right out front. Illegally parked and running! Like it was a big F.U. As if to say, 'no worries…this won't take long.' What a prick! At least they finally got to question him. But three months after she died…Geez!"

We talked about Lee and the possible outcomes of the investigation, and I told Sean all about Rick, Howard, and especially Joshua. Sean was a great listener and a great friend.

It didn't take long for the district attorney's office to call my family in to meet with them. I took the call and made the appointment for me, my mother and father to make the drive to Greensburg, PA to sit with the district attorney, Alan Slate, and the two investigating officers including Det. Hughes. The appointment was set for the following Wednesday.

Soon after that phone call I got an excited phone call from Brian Solomon. He informed me that he had brokered a deal with QVC. They wanted a spokesmodel for the product and since I was the package model and I now had some shopping channel experience, they wanted to meet with me. That meeting was set for Thursday, the day after I was to meet with the DA.

I drove alone to Greensburg with my bags packed for West Chester in the back seat. My plan was to meet with Alan Slate and his investigators and then immediately hit the road for QVC. It was such a strange mix of events, and it brought with it the same mix of emotions. More than anything, I drove to Greensburg with an intense sense of anticipation. No matter what the next few days were going to bring, things were moving and changing in my life in big ways and fast.

My parents met up with me in the courtyard in front of the county courthouse. I had dressed professionally for the meeting: a black pencil skirt, tall black pumps, a tan fitted blazer with a crisp white shirt underneath. I had also pulled my long hair back into a sleek ponytail and wore my small, rectangular, black-framed eyeglasses. Even at 30, I felt a little bit like a little girl playing businesswoman dress-up. We made our way through security and followed the signs to the district attorney's office.

The waiting area was much smaller than I would have imagined, and we announced our presence to the receptionist through a sliding glass window. Moments later, Det. Hughes opened the door to welcome us. After many phone conversations, I was happy to finally meet him in person. He wasn't at all what I had expected. He was a small man with sandy, blonde hair in his mid-forties. I had pictured a taller, darker, and more substantial man, but real Det. Hughes had a much softer and kinder look to him.

Det. Hughes shook all of our hands and asked us to follow him. He led us through a maze of rooms. We went down a hallway that had numerous filing cabinets and tables with files stacked high on them. It wasn't as organized as I would have imagined a district attorney's office being.

Almost sensing that feeling, Det. Hughes said, "Sorry about the mess. We're in the middle of a big case right now. Okay, here we are."

He led us into a conference room with a large wood conference table with many leather conference chairs around it. The room was lined with filled bookshelves. Now, this was what I was expecting a district attorney's office to look like. Just then, the door opened again, and Alan Slate came in followed by an additional investigator. Alan Slate was a tall, thin balding man with glasses. He was instantly recognizable to me from television campaign ads and signs as he had been the county's DA for years. The additional investigator was described as a "liaison between the Lower Burrell PD and the DA's office." He was a short, stout man with a full dark beard and almost angry looking dark eyes. He looked sloppy and more like a guy you would see sitting on a bar stool somewhere than an investigator.

We all said a brief 'hello' and took our seats at the tables. Det. Hughes took a seat down on the left side of the conference table near my parents and Mr. Slate and the other investigator sat near one another to the right. They all had files with them and immediately opened the manila folders when we sat. We all sat there silently for a moment, and I looked from side to side trying to catch the eye of any of them. They were all looking down.

Mr. Slate finally looked up. "I cannot express to you how sorry I am for the loss of your daughter, but…" It was the loudest *but* I had ever heard.

Det. Hughes and Mr. Slate took turns talking and at times reading directly from the interview with Lee. Det. Hughes detailed his notes about his long efforts to obtain an interview with Lee. All their talking combined into a swirl of words. All the talking added up to this: The case against Lee was purely circumstantial. The hardest part was that there was no clear cause of death. Camille would have to be exhumed, but to exhume her they would need a warrant which they couldn't get with the evidence they had. Plus, there hadn't been an exhumation case in Westmoreland County in over 25 years. They told my parents they would have a better chance of forcing the exhumation of her body on behalf of me and her children. We could state (as my mother pleaded in the hospital) that as her biological heirs, we had a right to know her cause of death. If we had her exhumed and any evidence was found, we could share it with them, but for now…there was nothing they could do.

It was so hard to hear that there was nothing they could do and that our search for answers was going to be turned back on our family to shoulder both the emotional and financial burden. My father would have to pay an attorney to fight for the exhumation and pay a coroner for the autopsy.

But I saw my father nodding and saying, "Done. I'll do it. We need to know."

I was ready to walk away from the meeting simply disappointed when the angry little sloppy investigator spoke up.

"I'm just going to say this, but I asked some people around Lower Burrell, and they said Lee isn't a bad guy…"

I pushed myself in my heavy leather chair back away from the table in disgust as he spoke.

"Listen," I interrupted. "You can tell me you don't have enough evidence to proceed. But how dare you sit there and tell me that he may be a nice guy! Who are you?"

"Lana…Lana," Det. Hughes said in a tone that said, 'please calm down.'

I rolled my eyes in disgust and walked out into the hallway. My parents followed.

We all walked out of the courthouse silently and deflated.

"You know, Mom, the truth always comes out. Did you even have yourself prepared for them telling us they had uncovered additional information that *proved* he murdered her? There's an enormous difference between suspecting and knowing," I said, trying to ease her mind and mine.

"I'll get the autopsy, and I will get Cyril Wecht to do it, but you have to be prepared, Marlene," my father said. "She's been gone for three months already, and God knows how much longer before this can happen. There may be nothing left of her to find any evidence."

The thought sickened me further and I excused myself. "I'm sorry, Dad. I really should get on the road. I have a five-hour drive ahead of me."

I kissed my mom on the cheek and headed to QVC Park.

This is not my life.

CHAPTER 27

Quality, Value, Convenience

If you have ever watched QVC, the word that I am sure comes to mind when you think of the hosts is perky. I had just been told by the district attorney that they were not going to proceed with the investigation of my sister's murder unless we had her body exhumed and autopsied. I had five children at home who were my responsibility. My marriage was nearly at an end and my house was in foreclosure.

Sure...I can do perky.

I used the five hours in the car to think and recenter myself. The drive to West Chester was really easy. It was basically a straight shot on the Pennsylvania Turnpike, and I passed the time listening to CDs and sometimes just riding in silence. I followed the directions straight to the hotel, a Holiday Inn Express, and checked in. I called home to check on the kids and Frankie was short with me as always. Brian called to make sure I had arrived safely and said he would pick me up the next morning at the hotel and drive me to QVC for our meeting with the buyer.

Brian picked me up the next morning and we headed to QVC Park. I never understood why they called it that until we pulled up. It was a massive collection of buildings sitting on a large park-like piece of land. We parked in Visitors Parking and walked across the walkway to the huge glass main doors. We checked in with security and they made badges with our names on them and led us back to one of the many conference rooms that lined the hallways. We sat for a moment waiting for the buyers to arrive.

"This buyer's a real bitch," Brian said. "She hates me."

"Gee, Brian. What'd you do, sleep with her?" I laughed.

"No. I told her she was stupid and didn't know how to do her job."

"Great," I said, shaking my head. "She's going to hate me by association!"

"No, no. She'll love you. Just be you."

Just then, the buyer walked in followed by a young intern. She was a sharp, middle-aged professional-looking woman; just the kind of woman who didn't buy the typical line of bullshit that Brian was used to selling. He was right, she hated him, and it was obvious.

They went back and forth about numbers, and I sat there smiling just trying to stay out of the crossfire. I could tell from the conversation the source of Brian's frustration. QVC has a buying policy that they only buy as much as they feel you can sell in a certain number of shows. Brian wanted them to order more, but the dismal sales didn't merit it. Here came the part I didn't know.

The buyer who hated Brian asked with ire in her voice, "Brian, Brian, Brian, *why* should I buy more? *What* is going to be *so* different about this time?"

"You're looking at it!" Brian pointed his finger at me.

I wanted to crawl under the table and die as the woman turned her eyes to me and shot me a prickly gaze. I smiled back at her with all the confidence that I *didn't* actually have. The woman hadn't actually even acknowledged my presence until then. She looked at me like she was examining a horse. I half expected her to come over and check my teeth.

She leaned in and said, "Talk to me, dear. How can you stand this man?"

"It takes a lot of practice and the patience of an elementary school teacher, but in time he grows on you. Once you realize you can tune him out it gets better. He really isn't that bad when he isn't speaking," I answered, shooting Brian a smirk and then looking directly back at her.

She stared at me for a second and then laughed. "Okay." She patted her hands together. "I like her. You, I still can't stand, but her I like."

I listened to them talk about me for the next few moments like I wasn't there.

"I'll have to see her tapes. She'll have to go through our training and get approved." Finally, the woman got up from the table and shook my hand. "Welcome to QVC. Good luck."

She patted Brian on the back and left the room with her intern trailing behind her like a maidservant.

"Bitch," Brian said under his breath.

I waited until we were in the parking lot to let Brian have it.

"What the fuck was that, Brian? I thought they *wanted* me. You just brought me in to save *your* deal. Now all the pressure is on *me* to sell all these extra towels."

"Yeah, but you're a superstar. You have no idea how great you are on television. You were so amazing in Toronto. You'll do it. I know you will. You'll thank me someday. This is a really big deal."

"No, Brian. I'm sorry. You're right. Thanks. I just wish you would've told me the truth."

I would have to wait until the next quarter to begin my shows. I was scheduled to train in June and my first shows would be scheduled for July. It was a bit unreal leaving there thinking that I would be out there working in the next few months. I was going to be a television co-host and spokesmodel on national television going live in front of an average viewership of three million people.

Certainly, this is not my life.

CHAPTER 28

Sybil

"I'll believe it when I see it," was Frankie's reply when I told him about my pending career as a television co-host.

For the entire seven years of our marriage, I couldn't go to the mall and not have to call home to inform him of where I was and when I would be coming home. It had gotten to a point where I just wouldn't want to go anywhere without him for too long out of irritation more than fear. Toronto, Nashville, and West Chester so close together had driven him into a complete shutdown. It's almost like when an object is moving so fast that it appears to not be moving at all; he was so mad that his response was a strange and scary nothingness.

He would make himself as scarce as possible. He wouldn't return home from work until late and after Sean had already left with the three other children. He would then take our boys to do something, to his parents, or outside being certain to exclude me. I would, in grateful exchange for his absence, not mention that he smelled of booze when he came home or that I found a large trash can full of empty beer cans in the garage. His drinking had always been a huge issue in our home, and it was always cyclical. He would start drinking or stopping at the bars after work occasionally. But then occasionally would turn into frequently and frequently would turn into every day.

On the days that I cared, I would drive by the two bars I was certain to find him at and drag him out or confront him about it when he came home. A huge fight would always ensue and would often end in him breaking something in a drunken rage or physically threatening me. He would never hit me, but he would use his size to intimidate me, bumping me with his chest or raising his fist as if to hit me but hitting something nearby instead. But now, that kind of drama was senseless to me. I simply ceased to care. One evening Jillian stopped in to see me and visit the boys. Frankie walked in all smiles and cheery, grabbing the boys and wrestling with them on the floor.

"Hi, Jillian," he said with a big smile as he chased Michael around the house. As he passed us running, Jillian leaned over and whispered, "My God, he reeks of booze!"

"I don't give a shit anymore, Jillian."

She gave me a look that said, "Wow, you really mean that."

I did. I really, really meant it.

It was mid-May now, and the days were getting longer and warmer. Frankie and I had settled into a strange peace that came with not really speaking to one another. In a couple of weeks, Camille's children would finish school, and Sean would be moving them to his home in Beaver Falls permanently.

On one of those evenings, Frankie and I were sitting on separate couches in the living room watching television when the telephone rang. It was past ten and the children were already in bed. In lieu of answering the phone, he leaned over and checked the caller ID.

"Washington. A telemarketer calling past ten? Fucking rude assholes!"

He silenced the phone and continued to watch the rest of the television program and then went to bed. I thought nothing of it and turned in for the night on the couch.

The next morning came, and all the children were now in the house running and playing after a 9:30 AM breakfast. The phone rang and I checked the caller ID, and it was Washington again.

Damn telemarketers, I thought and answered.

"Hello."

There was a brief pause and then an excited, "Hello, hello! How are you?"

I immediately recognized the voice. It was Joshua. My heart dropped hearing his voice so unexpectedly. I shuddered when I realized this was the phone call that had come through the night before and how close Frankie was to answering it.

"Is it okay that I called? Is this a good time for you?"

Just then, the gaggle of kids ran by me screaming and laughing and asking me questions. I answered their questions with my hand over the phone and then said, "As good as it gets, I guess, but…my husband almost answered the phone last night and…you know?"

Joshua and I had shared during our talks in Nashville how controlling our spouses were and how they didn't really welcome friends into our lives, especially those of the opposite sex. He understood what I was saying. He called under the guise of telling me that he got around to listening to my demo. He flattered me by telling me he was surprised at how good it was and that my contact information was on the demo, and he just called without really thinking. But he was really calling because of those shared issues with our spouses. He found a safe sounding board with me and he didn't want to give it up. I felt the same way.

This wasn't me. This wasn't my life.

May came to an end with screaming coming from my kitchen. It was the last day Camille's children would be spending every day at my house. Gabriel was having his preschool graduation and then they would move to Sean's permanently. My mother came over to help get the children ready and fixated on Nicole's messy hair. The boys all ran raucously around the house while my mother planted Nicole at my kitchen table to fix her hair. She began to scream the moment the brush touched her head. My mother had been in a complete fog since Camille died and the fog didn't lift as she continued to brush, oblivious to the ear-piercing screams. The boys were particularly rowdy that day, almost sensing this would be their last day together. They raised their voices to talk over Nicole's screaming. The house was deafeningly loud, but I watched my mother just obliviously brush away at Nicole's hair with a faraway look in her eyes. It all overtook me, and I walked out the back door.

On the back patio sat an empty beer cooler. I dragged it to the furthest point of the backyard, until I couldn't hear the screaming anymore, and sat on it. I buried my face in my hands and sat there rocking. I was torn. A big part of me was anxious for Camille's children to go and for my home to return to normal, but the other part of me was so sad to see them go and knew that there was no real normal to return to. Taking care of Camille's children kept her near me and the busyness they created prevented me from really grieving. It was like a pause button had been hit for five months and, sitting on a beer cooler in the backyard, someone hit play. I sat on the cooler sobbing and when I looked up, all the children and my mother were dead silent and peering out the kitchen window at me. I needed help.

Everyone I talked to asked me if I had *spoken to anyone about Camille's death*. I knew they were all alluding to therapy. I had put it off more because of financial and time constraints, but after I unraveled on a beer cooler, I finally agreed to go to a local psychologist. I had begun to have dreams that I was falling down a deep dirt sinkhole. Along the edges of the sinkhole were branches that looked like roots. I would grab onto a root and it would temporarily stop me from falling, but after a moment it would pull loose from the dirt, and I would go plummeting down again.

It didn't take much to figure out why I was having the dream, but I really wanted it to stop, and I really wanted to be able to tell people, "Yes. I got therapy," when they asked.

So, I made the appointment and drove myself to see someone.

I walked anxiously up the cement stairs of the house that was converted to an office for my first-ever therapy session. I was wearing jeans, high-heeled black boots, and a shirt with a long red scarf. On the way up the stairs the heel of my boot caught on the end of my long scarf, and I fell hard on the cement step. My knee took the brunt of the fall, and it ripped a huge hole in my jeans that within moments had blood pouring through it. I immediately got up and looked around in embarrassment to see if anyone had seen me make this klutzy move. It didn't seem so. I entered an empty waiting room and rang a buzzer by a door that was marked *Ring here upon entry*. I sat for a moment examining my knee. It was pretty banged up.

The therapist, an older man in his sixties with gray hair, opened the door. "Lana?"

"Yes." I jumped up and followed him back to his office.

He sat down in the wood-paneled room that was his office behind a large desk and asked me to sit in the chair on the other side of the desk facing him. "So, tell me why you are here today."

I think I started to cry the moment I started to speak.

"Alan died…Camille died…house gone…marriage ending… Nashville…murder investigation…stole a rabbit…affair…" I just babbled and cried and all the while I could see the therapist looking in bewilderment at my blood-soaked knee.

"Are you okay?" he asked, motioning to my knee.

"What, my knee? I'm fine. Well, my knee is fine."

"Do you want me to get you something for it?"

"What, my knee? No." *Forget about my fucking knee! Are you listening to me? My whole life is coming undone! I don't care about my damn knee!* Now, I am really, really hoping I just thought that and didn't say it out loud. Although it is possible that I may have, I sure hope I didn't.

What I do remember were the therapist's words to me.

"You are sad because you should be, and you are going to be for quite some time. You have had more tragedy happen to you in a short period of time than most see in a lifetime."

It felt so freeing to have someone give me permission to be sad. He went on to ask me more about my sister and I recalled to him stories about her. Then he leaned back in his chair and put his hands behind his head like he was thinking.

He looked at me with a fascinated look on his face. "You know…I have heard about this. But it usually occurs with twins. But you were same sex only siblings." He paused, thinking. "See, there is a phenomenon where when one twin dies, the other twin assimilates the deceased twin's personality. Some of the behavior you are exhibiting seems like it fits that mold. You are a people pleaser and caring for her children, befriending her friends, careless travel, brave and bold moves…all of it… sounds more like her behaviors than yours. I think it is possible that you have taken on aspects of your sister's personality to keep everyone happy, even you."

"Holy crap, I'm Sybil," I yelped.

CHAPTER 29

Single Mom

Michael was a colicky baby. He was the most pleasant baby in the world all day, until 7 PM hit. He would cry for three straight hours which felt more like an eternity. Frankie would swaddle him tight and walk in circles around the house endlessly bouncing and rocking him, but he wouldn't stop. He would finally stop crying and fall asleep in Frankie's arms, but the second Frankie would go to place him in his crib, he would wake and begin crying again. We would take turns throughout the evening trying to lull him to sleep, but Frankie was by far more patient. I was only 24 when I had Michael, and at the time it didn't seem that young. Now, I look at girls who are 24 and think, *how did I do that at their age? I was just a baby myself.*

I was convinced that something was wrong with Michael and would call my dad over to adjust his neck or whatever chiropractic magic he could muster up to fix him, because surely, he had to be sick with all of this crying. In one moment of exhaustion and frustration I handed Michael over to my dad and went stomping into my bedroom and threw myself on the bed. My father followed.

"I can't do this, Dad. I quit. I'm not good at it. Look, all he does is cry." I felt so terrible for even letting the words exit my mouth.

My dad kind of giggled to himself a little. "Honey, you're a mom now. You don't get to quit. You never get to quit. You never ever get to quit."

I think that moment was pivotal for me. Michael had only been around for a couple of months, and I don't think I understood completely what it meant to be a mother. I woke up and played with him, bathed him, changed him, cuddled him, and loved him. I was doing what I was supposed to be doing. But in my dad's words I realized that motherhood isn't about what you *do*, it is about what you *become*. Michael and then Aaron were as much a part of me as my arms or legs.

This was the weight that I carried with me into the decision to divorce Frankie. I knew that just like my arms or legs, wherever I went, they went. If I chose to stay in an unhealthy marriage, I would take them with me on that road. If I chose to leave Frankie, I would change the course of their lives forever. If I chose to stay with him, I handed the baton of tolerating verbal abuse down to another generation. I was torn. I thought of an analogy for life that Camille would often repeat.

"Hey, Lana. You know there's a safety monologue that flight attendants have to memorize to be able to give at the beginning of each flight. I stand up there and do it and I can see all of the people squirming and fidgeting and paying no attention. I wish they would because it contains one of life's little secrets," she said with a grin. "There's a part that I say when the oxygen masks drop…please place the mask on you first and then proceed to help children and loved ones." She continued mimicking the application of an oxygen mask. "See…you can't save anybody until you save yourself." So, feeling that I was not going to survive the dysfunction of my marriage another day, I put the mask on and asked Frankie for a divorce.

He fought me at first. But there was no stopping me, my mind was made up.

I moved out of the house that was in foreclosure and in with my parents. It was humbling, but necessary. I needed their help with the kids during my unpredictable QVC schedule. I needed help in a lot of ways.

Michael would sleep with Frankie when we were still together and I would sleep on the couch. Michael would start the evening off in his own bed, but Frankie would usually wake up each morning with Michael by his side. One evening, I woke to Michael hovering near my bed at my parents' house. He stood next to me with his blanket in his hand.

"Mommy, is Daddy ever coming back?" he asked with tears in his eyes. I couldn't bear to lie to him.

"No. He is not."

"Who will I sleep with?" he asked, his lip now quivering.

"Me." I pulled the blanket that was covering me up to welcome him.

He crawled up next to me and never asked me about the divorce again. I really thought it was going to be much harder than that, but it wasn't. It seems like the children, although deeply loving their father, acted with a sense of relief. I think they felt the tension between us much more than I ever knew.

Frankie and I established a fair custody settlement, the kids with me during the week and with him on the weekend. The children were amazingly resilient to the new schedule. I feared so deeply the effect a divorce would have on my children, but as closely as I watched, I couldn't see many changes. They seemed happy when they were with me and excited to go with their father on the weekends.

I busied myself through August and September, going back and forth to West Chester to do my QVC spots, learning to adapt as a single mom and trying to enjoy my newfound freedom. I could go shopping with my mother without the nervousness of being gone too long for Frankie's liking. I remember one Saturday my mother and I got caught up in looking at a new line of jewelry at Macy's; trying it on, looking for matching pieces, and showing it to one another.

My mother looked at her watch. "Wow. It's 7 o'clock already. Should we get home?"

I thought for a second.

"No…no. We don't have to go. We can stay as long as we want," I said with a smile.

This was not my life. Not the one it had been.

CHAPTER 30

The Autopsy Report

I was in my father's office when the autopsy report arrived. I was in the back room with him when his secretary appeared with a thick manila envelope that had just arrived by registered mail. My father signed for it and quickly opened the package. He pulled out the thick report and began to read it.

"What does it say, Dad? Tell me."

My heart was in my stomach. Was I ready to hear something terrible? Was I ready for this today? Either way, it didn't matter. The report was there, and I was going to have some answers, finally. Or so I thought.

My father just held his head and then in a moment of frustration he pounded his fist on the table and got up and left the room. I followed him as he went to the telephone in the hallway and dialed.

"Lee, this is Joseph. I have the autopsy report and Camille did NOT die of a heart attack. Do you hear me? She did not!" Then he just started to cry and hung up the phone.

I was so confused and I grabbed the report and began to read. When you do an exhumation, a family member has to be there to identify the body. My father insisted it had to be him. He was definitely right. Neither my mom or I could have handled that additional trauma.

The first thing that struck me was that Cyril Wecht had described the level of decomposition of my sister as extensive. My father told us that she looked nearly untouched, even beautiful. I knew he was lying to make us feel better, but that proved it. The rest of the report was a mix of medical jargon, some I understood perfectly and others I didn't.

The report stated that my sister's heart was perfect; in fact they determined her age as 25 by the condition of her body and internal organs. Camille would have liked that. Her heart was perfect. There was no "massive heart attack" as Lee had said over and over again.

But her one lung was saturated with blood clots, so much so that it weighed twice the weight of the other one.

My father's next call was to Dr. Wecht's office.

"What would cause blood clots at this level?" he asked when he was finally able to reach Dr. Wecht. I watched and waited for the answers as my dad spoke to him and nodded and then shook his head in disbelief. My father got off the phone and said, "Well, I'm sorry, but there's no way to know how your sister died."

I felt the blood drain from my body.

"What?"

"Look, there were blood clots in her lungs. That killed her. There's no doubt about that, but what caused the clots, especially at the level they found, there's no telling."

"What does Cyril Wecht think could have caused that?"

"Poison could have, but he didn't find anything in her system. That would just be speculation and nothing that would ever hold up in court. She lay for several days dying. She was buried and decomposing for months. I told you this could happen. If it was poison, it very well could have metabolized out of her body even before her death. All they tested for in the hospital was street drugs and of course found nothing. I told you this could happen. There's no proof. It's over."

The autopsy created more questions than answers. I couldn't believe it. That was it. Without fanfare or ceremony, the murder investigation was over. With no clear cause of death, the investigators would not continue the case.

It felt like Camille had died all over again. I wanted answers. I wanted justice. I wanted a lot of things that it was clear now I wasn't ever going to get. At that moment, my parents and I were sentenced to a lifetime of wondering.

I would never be able to simply answer the question, "So, how did your sister die?"

I don't think people understand the gravity of that. I will never, ever know. My parents will never, ever know. Her children will never, ever know. The depth and finality of that fact was as hard to wrap my mind around as her death.

This is not my life.

I wasn't wishing that the autopsy report would have proved that Lee murdered her. In fact, I braced myself for that possibility with great sadness. I didn't want to know that my sister's final moments were looking into the face of a man she believed loved her as he injected her with some kind of poison and that he stood over her as her lungs filled with blood, gasping for air, and pleading for help. But what that man

did to my family by refusing the initial autopsy and his suspicious behaviors in the weeks and months prior to her death was to never erase
that as a possibility for me and my family.

Of all the things that Lee stole from Camille's children and my family
– the house, car, clothes, jewelry, furniture, savings – our inability to
definitively answer that question was his greatest theft and I hated him
more in that moment than my spirit could bear.

CHAPTER 31

Too Many Country Songs

I already had my return trip to Nashville scheduled for the week following the results of the autopsy report. Once again, the trip was coming at a perfect time to get away. But I wasn't the same girl stepping off the airplane into the sunny, bright airport as I was the year before. In the year between, I had gotten divorced and became a television personality. Mentally, I wasn't the sad little "Nashville virgin." This time I was filled with anger to the point where it stood me up straight and could be easily confused with confidence. I was a woman on a mission... except I didn't really have a mission to speak of. All I knew is that I was desperate to see Joshua again. My love for him had eclipsed my love for music.

The NSAI Convention had been moved that year to the Millennium Maxwell House, a larger and more opulent hotel with an enormous lobby. I pulled my bags through the lobby to the reception desk and reached into my carry-on bag for my ringing cell phone. It was Joshua.

"Turn around," he almost sang.

I turned to see him, Rick, and Howard right behind me. I dropped my bags and hugged Rick, then Howard, then Joshua. Joshua held on tighter and longer than he should have, and it didn't go unnoticed. Howard or Rick had no idea that we had been talking daily over the last year. For all they knew, we were all meeting up again as we had promised the prior year. But neither man was stupid, and they could tell very quickly that Joshua and I knew each other much better than we should have.

Little things we now knew about each other were slipping out through our group conversations and it didn't take long for Rick to pull me aside and ask what was going on.

"We're just friends," I lied.

The truth was that we had somehow crossed the line. Our phone calls started as what felt like a safe place to complain about our marriages and the struggle of trying to make something of your life with a resistant spouse. That led to conversations about life in general and that's where things got tricky. We talked about our childhoods. He was quite different and interesting to me. He was one of seven siblings. Big families always intrigued me as mine was small and ever shrinking. We talked about our love of music and would share song ideas over the phone and would honestly critique one another. I filled him in on the gory details of my sister's death and he listened with compassion and interest. We talked about our children and how much we loved them. We talked about our pets, friends, and the weather. Before we knew it, nothing happened in either of our lives without us sharing it.

Joshua was driving the rental SUV and Howard tried to let me sit up front with him, but I refused and sat in the back seat with Rick. Joshua tried to pick up the check at dinner, but I insisted on paying for my portion. It was dinner for five this time: me, Joshua, Rick, Howard, and the big, fat elephant in the room. The familiarity that Joshua and I had forged over the phone had generated the opposite effect once we were together again in person. We were working hard to keep our distance from one another, to not look suspicious, which just made us look more suspicious. It was exhausting! We opted to turn in at a decent hour that night so that we could be rested and ready for the convention that was to begin early the next morning. I also think Rick and Howard couldn't wait to get Joshua alone to get to the truth.

This year, the room was set up with a large round table and there was breakfast being served. We all began to talk and eat as the room swirled with people arriving and mingling. One by one, people would approach our table and fill the six empty seats.

Then a voice blasted with a deep, thick Southern drawl as if it was coming through a loudspeaker. "Good Lord! You are one extraordinary looking woman!"

I looked around to see where the voice was coming from. Hovering right next to my chair was the source of the comment, Mr. Jimmy St. John. It was immediately apparent that this guy was a character and more character than guy. He stood there, slightly overweight and in his mid-forties with a baby face, wearing jeans, a T-shirt, and a tuxedo jacket. His most distinguishing feature was a head of coal, black hair that may or may not have been a hairpiece.

I honestly didn't know how to respond to him. So, I just kind of half grinned at him.

It was strange being seen for just me in this new place, even if that 'me' was just my appearance. After months of being the grieving sister, the frustrated wife, the overwhelmed mother, there was something oddly freeing about being reduced to simply how I looked. I wasn't sure if I should be flattered or annoyed, so I settled somewhere in between.

It seemed that everyone in the room knew Jimmy. They were all approaching him, shaking his hand, and giving him hugs. I could hear every word of his conversations with them because he planted himself right next to the empty chair beside me. He stood and talked with his hand on the chair. I gathered from overheard conversations that he was a regular songwriter around town and was there to be one of the expert panelists for the convention. Every time someone would come up to talk to him, he would say, "I'm sorry. Have you met my wife?" He would then motion his hand in my direction. I would just sit there wide-eyed. He would let out a thunderous laugh and say, "Oh. She isn't my wife, yet. But the day has just begun."

Rick and Howard found it amusing, but Joshua would squirm in his seat every time he would say it and roll his eyes. I just kind of smiled and went with the flow. Jimmy seemed harmless. I could tell this was a role he was playing. Big, bold, and brash was his schtick and you could tell that he was well-known and well-liked. There would be moments when someone you could tell knew him better than the rest would approach him, and he would stop and talk normally, dropping the act and his voice to the point of normal. As the head of the NSAI called out over the microphone for everyone to take their seats, Jimmy plopped down in the seat next to me. "Jimmy St. John," he said, extending his hand to me first and then to all around the table in introduction.

"Lana what?" he asked.

"Kennedy," I replied using my given name, which felt weird after eight years of using my married name.

"St. John?" he replied.

"Kennedy," I answered, shaking my head.

"You really are extraordinary," he said again, this time more earnestly.

"So, I've heard. So has *everybody* else in the room."

Jimmy invited us to a CD-Release party at a studio on Music Row that evening. He told us to just tell the guy at the door that he told us it was okay to come. Nobody should have been more excited than Joshua. He had already recorded his second album in Nashville and was still trying to get signed to another record deal. This party was a big opportunity for him more than measly songwriters like me, Rick, and Howard. But he was annoyed that the invitation was for me and my "entourage" as Jimmy had nicknamed the three of them throughout the day.

"He likes you, ya know?" Joshua said in the car on the ride over.

Before I could answer, Rick and Howard answered in my defense. "She's a big girl. She can take care of herself."

"He's harmless," I chimed in from the back seat.

We went to the party and had a blast. The studio was crowded with people, and it was a good hour before Jimmy even found us there. He spotted and acknowledged the whole group of us.

"Hey. You made it! Have a drink, have fun!" He grabbed my hand and kissed it. "Mrs. St. John." But then he disappeared into the crowd for the rest of the evening.

"I told you he was harmless," I whispered through the crowd to Joshua.

He turned and gave me a face that said, "whatever."

CHAPTER 32

Nighttime Crowe

Our posse grew even larger the next day. We met a fun married couple who both wrote music and they invited us to an evening barbeque. We followed the directions to their house in a residential area on the outskirts of Nashville. It was a lovely but modest house set on a large piece of land and it was crowded with people. There was a fire lit in the backyard, and it seemed everyone there had a guitar hanging from their back.

As the sun began to set, we gathered in a circle around the fire and people pulled out their guitars and started to play. Spontaneously, someone there would start to sing along. They sang covers of old songs and some brand-new ones. It was magical to listen to all of this talent in one place. I relished the laid-back atmosphere of artists feeling free to express their feelings and couldn't help envisioning myself living there again.

As the guitars passed from hand to hand around the fire, each song-writer reaching for something personal to share, I found myself think-ing of those quiet evenings at the piano with Camille. She never had my musical ability, but she had an ear for what worked. 'That one,

Lana,' she'd say when I'd stumble upon a melody that moved her. Now, surrounded by these Nashville strangers pouring their hearts into songs, I understood what I was really doing here – trying to find the melody that might carry the weight of everything left unsaid between us. Something beautiful enough to honor her, honest enough to hold my anger at being left behind.

Jimmy introduced us to Simon Crowe at the barbeque. Simon was an extremely cute, but small guy. He had dusty blonde hair with a cut that looked very modern and expensive and wore jeans and a shirt that was very trendy.

Simon Crowe and I struck up a conversation.

"You with that guy?" he asked, nodding his head in Joshua's direction.

"No. Why does everyone keep asking that? We're friends."

"Does *he* know that?"

"He's married."

"Does *he* know that? Look. He's looking over here now. He's keeping an eye on you."

There was something about Nashville that made me visible in a way I hadn't been in years. Back home, I was defined by my relationships – Camille's sister, Frankie's wife, the boys' mother. Here, these men saw something else. I wasn't sure what exactly, but at least it was something of my own, even if they were reading me all wrong.

Simon and I sat and talked for a while. He actually lived right next door to the couple and asked if I would play some of my stuff on the piano at his house. I politely refused. I was naïve, but not dumb. I knew the moment I would be alone with Simon he would be all over me.

Jimmy came up to me laughing. "I heard you shot down the Daytime Crowe! That doesn't happen much around here."

"Daytime Crowe?"

"Oh yeah, there's a Nighttime Crowe and a Daytime Crowe. You'll see. Stay away from Nighttime Crowe."

Sure enough, at a party on 12th and Porter the next evening, I ran into Nighttime Crowe while coming out of the bathroom. It was back around a dark corner of the bar. I opened the bathroom door and there stood Nighttime Crowe. "You again!" he slurred. "My God, woman. You are perfect like a porn star."

That supposed compliment is still one of the stupidest things I have ever heard come out of a man's mouth and I've heard a LOT of stupid things come out of men's mouths.

"Why don't you like me?" he slurred again putting his hands on my shoulders.

"Um..." I struggled to find the words to shoot him down but not offend him. "I like you, Simon..." I tried to move my shoulders to shake his hands free.

"Yeah." He tightened his grip before I could even finish what I was saying. "You do?"

Before I could mutter another word, he pushed me up against the wall with the strength of a wrestler and tried to kiss me.

I turned my head to the side. "Hey, that's enough."

When he wouldn't release his grip around my arms, I started to panic. Just then, Joshua came walking around the corner. At first, he almost turned as if he had walked in on a mutual embrace, but once he saw that I was trying to push Simon off he grabbed the back of his shirt, freeing me from his grip, and then slammed him up against the wall.

"What are you doing?! Get off her!" He pushed Simon in the chest.

I stepped in between, not to protect Simon, but to stop Joshua from getting into a fight. "It's fine. Nighttime Crowe's going home and sleeping it off, right?"

Simon just stood there looking drunk and stupid.

I pulled Joshua back to the booth where our large group was sitting. My mom's voice rang in my head.

Deny, defend, avoid.

I felt unsteady as we made our way back to the booth. My hands gripped the edge of the table as I sat down, trying to regain my composure. For a moment, Simon's aggressive advance had pulled me right out of Nashville and back into that helpless feeling I'd been fighting against since Camille died, since I was a little girl letting herself become invisible to keep the perception of peace. I took a deep breath. I was tired of being caught off guard by other people's actions, tired of having to react rather than choose. Camille would have knocked Simon out like a playland employee, not waited to be rescued by Joshua. I was not his to protect. I was tired of being the Damsel, I wanted to be the Knight. I wanted to be Camille.

"Well, Jimmy, I just met Nighttime Crowe," I said, trying to make light of it.

"You could have told her he turned into a deranged rapist when he drinks. He just attacked her outside the bathroom," Joshua said, directing his anger at Jimmy.

"It's over. It's fine," I said to both Jimmy and Joshua.

Jimmy went back at Joshua, "Look, all I meant was that he turns into a real asshole when he drinks. I never thought he would do something like that. Look, the guy is used to getting what he wants. Your girlfriend here just has him all wound up 'cause she shot him down."

"I'm not his girlfriend," I mumbled.

The whole thing was becoming too much of a scene for me.

"Just drop it, okay?" I said to both of them.

The rest of the group tried to change the subject, but Joshua sat there angry for the rest of our time at 12th and Porter. The elephant was growing out of control.

CHAPTER 33

Some Stories Don't Get an End

We had one more night in Nashville. The night started again with dinner. Jimmy offered to take us all to a great local Mexican restaurant, and maybe because it was my last night in Nashville, or maybe it was for courage, but I started drinking margaritas…lots of margaritas. Jimmy then without warning decided to slay the elephant right there at the dinner table.

"Okay, let me get this straight. You're married." He pointed at Howard. "You're married." He pointed at Rick. My stomach dropped as I sensed exactly where he was going with this. "And you're married?" He pointed to Joshua. "But you're not married to her? She's divorced from Pittsburgh." He waved his hands like an attorney making a case. "So… how does married in Seattle come to love divorced from Pittsburgh?"

Everyone sat slack-jawed from the bold question. All I could think was thank God I'm drunk. I couldn't sit through this sober. Joshua just sat there stunned. He tried to answer, but all that came out was, "Ba…ba…I don't…I don't…I don't…know." He cradled his head in his hands and then wiped his hands down over his face in exacerbation.

Jimmy took mercy on him. "Aww...we all love divorced from Pittsburgh, huh?"

Rick and Howard nodded, and they all changed the subject, but Joshua just sat there looking pale. What Jimmy couldn't understand was that grief creates its own gravity. Joshua and I had both lost something essential – me, my sister; him, his musical dreams. We recognized in each other that peculiar hunger that comes from having a piece of yourself torn away. Camille would have called it fate and would have seen our connection as destiny. I just saw it as two people finding temporary shelter in the same storm.

We left dinner and moved the party to a nearby bar that was having an open mic night, not mentioning stumbling over his words at dinner when it came to loving me. We were meeting several of the other friends we had met throughout the week there.

"Bring your guitars, boys. We're gonna put on a show tonight," Jimmy exclaimed out of his car window to ours as we reached the parking lot.

"Clearly, we need to talk," I whispered to Joshua on the way in. He nodded in agreement. But the group swirling around us made it impossible at the moment.

Joshua worked hard to avoid me, but Jimmy looked for the first opportunity to corner me. "So, what the hell are you thinking?" he said, putting a fresh ice-cold beer down in front of me.

I picked it up and had a drink. "I don't think I'm thinking right now. I needed someone, I guess. I don't know. It really isn't like me. I don't hurt people, you know? I'm a terrible person."

"You shouldn't be too hard on yourself. Damn, I've seen these kinds of things happen down here a million times in the 20 years I've been livin' here." Then his eyes got wide. "Okay...it's time to shake this place up!"

He grabbed his guitar and motioned Joshua and Howard to follow him as he made his way to the stage. Howard shook his head "no" but Joshua looked excited and grabbed his guitar and quickly followed. The owner of the bar, an old gray-haired man who looked more aging hippie than country, was emceeing the open mic night.

When he saw Jimmy approaching, guitar in hand, the owner of the club grabbed the mic and spoke to the crowd. "Well, we have a treat tonight folks! Jimmy St. John's going to bring some soul to the house. Now, who you got with ya Jimmy?"

Jimmy jumped up onto the stage and grabbed the microphone. "I got married in Seattle here." He slapped Joshua on the back.

Joshua did not look amused by the nickname, but he let out a small smile trying to play along.

Jimmy took a small step back and he and Joshua fiddled with their guitars tuning them. Then Jimmy grabbed the mic and said, "This one is for one *extraordinary* woman!"

Jimmy began to sing. His voice was deep and gravely, and his style was straight up Southern Blues. Most of all, Jimmy was loud.

"Gotta be loud in this town," I recalled him saying as he sang.

I am going to admit that I am not a big blues fan, but he was good and very entertaining to watch. The song dedicated to me was one of his originals and the gist of the song was about a "hot" woman. Rick and Howard and the rest of the group hooted and hollered as Jimmy went through the song, every once in a while inserting "Lana" when it applied. Instead of "the woman was so irresistible," he would sing, "and Lana was so irresistible." Then my whole group would laugh. I was a little embarrassed, but it was all in good fun. Jimmy finished the song and the crowd went wild with applause.

Then it was Joshua's turn. He grabbed the mic and mimicked Jimmy's accent. "This is for that same *extraordinary* woman."

He went on to sing his original upbeat and straight-up country song, *You Got Me*, which is about no matter how hard a guy tries to figure his life out, it still keeps adding up to "you." I think both Jimmy and the crowd were stunned for a moment at how good he was. He more than held his own with Jimmy. In fact, he kind of showed him up.

It all went downhill from there. I think Jimmy's ego kicked in, and Joshua's jealousy. They went back and forth three times. Each time they would direct the song at me. I went from being oddly flattered to wishing it would end and end fast.

And again, I thought, *This is not my life. I'm not the girl who has two singers on stage battling for her attention.*

"Can we go?" Joshua asked immediately at the end of the set. He looked at me completely stone-faced.

"Sure," I said, knowing he was really mad.

We motioned to Rick and Howard, and we all said quick goodbyes to all and left. We all sat silently as Joshua drove; the tension was thick.

"Are you mad at me?" I asked.

"You know, that's not her fault," Rick added.

"He was just messing with you a little, Josh. It's nothing to get bent out of shape about," Howard chimed in.

"It was actually a pretty good show…" Rick continued, trying to make small talk.

But Joshua interrupted. "Stop! Just everyone stop. Fuck!"

He slammed his palms on the steering wheel. We drove the rest of the way to the hotel in silence. We walked through the lobby quietly and all got on the elevator together. Then, I just started to cry. I was trying to hold it in but tears just streamed down my face. Rick was standing next to me and when he saw me crying, he looked angry.

"You know what, Joshua, most of life is a joke to me. But one thing I hate is when people are selfish."

Joshua was standing with his back to us and started to say, "I'm not being selfish!" But as he spun around, he saw me crying and his face dropped.

The elevator door opened to my floor. I went to squeeze by Joshua, but he grabbed my elbow. I turned around to see Rick and Howard standing side-by-side behind Joshua. With Joshua still holding onto my elbow, Rick reached out and pushed Joshua off the elevator.

I turned just as the door was closing on Rick and Howard. They both raised up their right hands like Native Americans saying "how" and the door closed on them to leave me and Joshua alone in the quiet hotel hallway.

He freed my arm, and we stared at each other's faces for a moment until I turned to walk down the hall in the direction of my room.

He followed. "I'm not mad at you. It's just hard. This is a ridiculous situation, and I don't even know how we got here."

I reached my room and turned my back to the door and slid down to the ground. I sat on the floor, leaning up against the door looking up at him.

"I don't know how I got here either." The tears welled back up in my eyes because I was quite sure how.

Joshua, taking a cue from me, slid down the wall across the hall and sat with his knees up and his arms resting lazily on top.

"I think you came along when I needed someone, but not just anyone," I said. "I needed you. Someone who wasn't grieving, someone who understood me but didn't know me before, someone who didn't have any expectations of me. I didn't want to be me anymore when I met you. But I am me…kind of…fuck, I don't really know anymore. Maybe the therapist was right. Maybe Lana died that night, too…right along with Camille."

Joshua was raised deeply religious. That type of upbringing led him to marry at 22 to the first and only girl he was ever with. My reasoning for entering into an affair with him was much more complex than his; he simply wanted something different. He wanted to see and experience someone new. He never admitted that to me, but as he sat there on the floor of the hotel hallway at 4:00 AM looking at a family picture that he pulled from his wallet and sobbing, he didn't need to tell me. I knew.

"I don't know who you were. I just know who you are now and that is someone I love," he said through tears. "I really do. I don't know how or when it turned, but it did. I wanted to beat the shit out of that guy for pushin' on you at the bar. I wanted to deck Jimmy right on stage for singing to you. Do you know what I thought to myself the first moment I saw you? I thought, there's the woman I'm meant to be with. I don't feel like that for my wife, and I should! She's never been anything but good to me. She's the mother of my kid…oh, my son… oh…" He continued to sob and rub at the picture of his family.

I was now holding my knees and rocking with tears streaming down my face. "What have I done? What have I done?"

I knew Joshua was falling for me. I could hear it in the tone of his voice during our talks. I could hear it in his excitement when I picked up. But I was falling for him, too, and I only cared about myself. How horrible! I only cared about myself and my own grief and what I needed to make myself feel better.

"You know, Joshua, the night before I met you last year I watched *The Bridges of Madison County*. Have you ever seen it?"

He wiped his face with his sleeve and quietly said, "Yes."

"At first when I read the book, I thought she was a whore, a glorified cheater. Then that night, I thought she was stupid for not running after Robert Kincaid and yelled at the television for her to get out of the damn truck and go after her love!"

Joshua looked across the hall and straight into my eyes. "And now?"

"And now I don't think anything is that simple. Things are rarely black and white and that was a statement I used to think only assholes said to justify their mistakes."

I stood up and put my hand on the door to my hotel room. I fumbled through my purse and pulled out the swipe card to unlock it. As I swiped the key I continued. "But you...you, need to *stay* in the truck."

I could barely look back at him and could only glance at him from the corner of my eye.

He remained seated and began to cry again. He covered his eyes. "Okay, but how am I supposed to do that? How do I just let you go now? It seems so unfinished, empty...like a book you stop reading right in the middle of the damn thing."

I held onto the hotel room door tightly, resisting the overwhelming urge to go to him and comfort him. I then felt the warmth of his breath on my neck. He had risen to stand right behind me at the door. I couldn't turn around. His hand touched my waist and he pulled me close.

I reached down and reluctantly pulled his arms off my waist.

"Don't do anything you'll regret," he whispered in my ear as I grasped the hotel room door and swiped my key.

"That's what I'm trying to do." I entered the room alone and closed the door on Joshua forever.

CHAPTER 34

Peace

My best friend Jillian converted from Catholicism to an open-Bible, Pentecostal church. She would often urge me to attend church with her on Sundays and I would go, now and again. The small church was an oddly perfect fit for her. She found warmth and love amongst the vivacious and faith-filled congregation. I turned down Jillian's many invitations to join her at church in the year after my sister's death.

I wasn't mad at God. But I would often think of the cliché saying, "I know God won't give me anything I can't handle, I just wish He didn't trust me so much." I wasn't ready to face Him. Why *did* He trust me so much?

I decided it was time for me to find out, and upon my return from Nashville, I finally took Jillian up on her offer.

We entered the tiny church, and the choir was invited up to sing. A good 75% of the congregation was in the choir and it left little Jillian and me to feel like we were getting our own, private concert. The power of their strong gospel voices shook the room. I could feel my lips begin to tremble and my nose start to burn. My nose burning was always a telltale sign that tears were on their way. My chest tightened and I took deep breaths to try to stop it, but their voices shook me. I sat and fought the urge inside of me to get up and run out of the church. I needed to feel this. I finally succumbed to the emotion and the tears streamed down my face.

At the end of the singing, as always, they invited anyone who wanted to be 'prayed on' to come to the front of the church. I was raised in churches similar to this, but going to the front of the church was always too embarrassing for me. I found it a moving and powerful display, but I was always too shy to go.

Jillian looked over at me with the streams of tears running down my face and gently took my hand and said, "Let's go."

She had clearly filled in her friends at the church on my troubles and had asked them all to pray for me because the second I reached the front of the church they surrounded me.

The pastor laid his hands on my head and prayed. "Lord Jesus, this girl has suffered so much loss, more loss than some of us can imagine."

"Amen," called out one parishioner.

"But we know you have not left her. Be with her Jesus. Comfort her."

"Comfort her, Jesus," yelled another parishioner.

"He has not left you, my girl. Talk to Him, ask Him for what you need. Ask Him for what you need from Him today and He will answer."

I felt put on the spot. What *did* I want? What did I *want?*

The pastor's wife grabbed my tear-soaked face and cupped it in her hands. "Sweet girl, what do you want?"

I answered her with the first word that came to my mind and with tears running down my face, I said, "Peace."

Peace is a funny thing. It only comes when you ask for it.

I focused on my career and building a new life. Since beginning at QVC, I managed to double the sales each and every year I was there. The producers track your sales on a line graph in real time. The graph would climb off the charts each time I did an on-air, even on the slowest of sales nights. It earned me the nickname "Spike" amongst the staff and crew. Getting a new nickname at 32 amused me.

I met Chuck Woolery when he was there selling socks on the time slot right after mine. He was a nice guy, and I was a little giggly because I used to watch his old dating show, The Love Connection, every night in college before I went to bed.

On another night, I sat and complained about the immaturity of men with a nice, curly-haired man wearing horn-rimmed glasses. I didn't recognize him as Anson Williams, Potsie Weber from Happy Days, until he went on-air to sell some kind of face exercising thing.

I came home from one show to have Aaron, now four years old, mad at me.

"Mommy, I waved at you, and you didn't wave back!" he said, pouting.

Instead of explaining how a television worked, I started all my shows from that point on with a little wave, just for Aaron. Most of all, I told the stories of my experiences to anyone who asked. They were my stories. They were all mine.

For the next two years, I kept moving and working and breathing in and out. A day would go by and at the end of it I would think, *I almost made it through the day without missing my sister, without thinking about her.* Of course, then I would think, *well, I just did…so, there goes that!*

Camille's children settled into their home in Beaver Falls with Sean and he became the most active father I have ever seen. They got involved with so many athletic and academic activities that it is hard to keep track. The children showed me tiny pieces of their mother that were both comforting and heartbreaking. Mitchell developed into an excellent student, just like his mother. Gabriel became the feisty and driven one with a look in his eyes at all times like he is up to something, just like his mother. Nicole bloomed into the perfect likeness of her mother, but with dark hair. One day when she was visiting my parents' house, she sat at the kitchen table and let out a big sigh.

"What's the matter, Nicole?" I asked her.

"It's tough being a little girl without a mommy." She sighed. My heart ached as she continued. "I can't remember what she looks like. My dad says that if I want to see her, I should look at you, Aunt Lana."

"I think that works both ways, Nicole." I held back my tears. "You can look at me to see your mommy and I can look at you to see my sister. Is that a deal?"

She got up and wrapped her tiny arms around me. "Deal."

Sean doesn't speak much of Camille anymore. I think it will always be too painful for him. He continues to love Camille through the meticulous care of their children. Every year on Camille's birthday, he takes the kids to do something special. He says he does that to honor her life, but he does that already by taking on the awesome responsibility of raising three small children alone. He was also finally able to fall in love again. He remarried a pediatrician with three children of her own. They are like a smarter and calmer Brady Bunch and when I watch him with her, there is a peace that he never had with Camille. He deserves that.

My mother and father…sigh…I wish I could put a bow on it. But it was like the volumes of their underlying souls were turned up. Mom carried herself through her days with grace, kindness and a deep burning sadness. Dad, on the other hand, carried his anger like a badge he felt he had earned. I wanted them both to have a moment when they saw Camille's death as a realization that life was too short for sadness and anger, but we all get a story to write and that wasn't theirs. It was mine.

As for Lee, Sean called me, infuriated three years after Camille's death.

"That son of a bitch is now coming after the kids' Social Security money!"

I have never through all of it heard Sean so furious. During Camille's time at Delta, she had paid into Social Security enough for her children to be collecting a modest monthly amount. Sean made a nice living and was putting that money into an untouched "future fund" for them for college or whatever they may need when they got older. It would be a gift from their mother when they reached a certain age. Lee decided to try to come after that money by claiming that Camille was the primary breadwinner in the home and claiming rights to that money on behalf of his daughter.

His rationale behind that claim was that she was president of his company. His crazy statement in her obituary NOW made sense. He was setting this up. His daughter had a living mother who paid child support. It was a ridiculous claim, but we had to take it to trial. We all pulled together to face him in the hearing. He walked into the small courtroom in the Social Security Department with his attorney Sammy Blackburn. We just had to prove that Camille was furloughed as a flight attendant during their short marriage. In that, I was the star witness, as I was testifying to our long phone conversations and that at no time was she working or acting as president of his company.

Sean's attorney, Pete McCallister, a young, energetic fellow, had been filled in on the whole story behind this case. He knew how important this was to my family and faced the case with the intensity of a murder trial. He was prepared for the trial with expert witnesses and pictures and most of all tax records of Lee's income. He pulled out the pre-nuptial agreement in which Lee had stated he was a millionaire. He then pulled out the Social Security paperwork in which he claimed to only have made $25,000 the year they were married. He had subpoenaed Lee's tax returns for the last five years and the judge was furious when he found out they were not delivered and asked all of us except the attorneys to leave the room. He gave Lee's attorney a tongue lashing for the delay. The hearing went on for hours. Finally, it was my turn to testify.

Pete turned to me. "You're on. Relax, please."

I sat just inches away from Sammy and Lee. Lee once again avoided all eye contact.

Sammy immediately went on the attack. "Isn't it true you have a vendetta against my client, and you would be willing to say anything to ensure he loses today! Isn't it true you and your family accused my client of murdering your sister?"

The judge began to bang his gavel and yelled, "Mr. Blackburn! Mr. Blackburn! Stop!"

Sammy was leaning up into my face trying to elicit an emotional reaction from me. Instead, through the yelling of the judge for him to stop, I simply said, "Your client was investigated for murdering my sister. I accused him of nothing. His suspicious actions brought us to doubt him and today does little to ease that."

I gave my story with conviction and composure. In the final ruling that came months later, the judge ruled in Sean's favor and gave some scathing advice to Lee to stop all attempts to come after Camille's children's money. It was a small but monumental victory. I decided at that moment that justice always comes, but it isn't my job to be the judge.

Whatever the truth of my sister's death may be, it *will* come out someday. Until then, I needed to live my life. My life…it was a strange concept to me.

CHAPTER 35

The Last Ride

The sets at QVC were decorated for the Christmas season. I wrapped my segment and exited to the Green Room to gather my things. I waved to everyone there who had become a second family to me after the years of shows.

Moving into the changing room, I saw a new girl sitting there looking terrified. As I kicked off my spiky heels and pulled my sweats and pullover out of my bag, I looked over to her and said, "Don't be nervous. Believe in the product and believe in yourself and you'll do great."

"It's live television. I'm freaked out."

I pulled my makeup remover wipes out of my bag and wiped away the mask of stage makeup and zipped up my bag as her pager went off to alert her that she needed to report to the set.

"Swim or die!" I yelled to her as she exited the room.

I raced down the winding corridors in comfortable clothes for the drive home. I opted out of staying in the hotel to drive through the night to make it home in time to get to Michael's Christmas concert. Reaching the large glass vestibule, I stopped at the reception desk to toss my security pass.

"Lana, wait…this came for you." The receptionist handed me a padded envelope.

I pushed on the padding and felt something hard and square inside.

"Hmm…thanks," I said, thinking it odd because I rarely got mail sent to me there. "See you in a few days."

I rushed to my car, tossed my wardrobe bag in the back seat and the envelope in the passenger side and stared at it for a minute. I started my car to warm it up, the exhaust creating a cloud in the dark West Chester night. Then I leaned over and grabbed the package, delicately tearing it open. There he was. Joshua. Leaning up against a fence in a white cowboy hat and jeans on the cover of his new CD. A yellow sticky note in his handwriting simply read, "Track 7."

I took a deep breath and closed my eyes for a second. It had been years, and the sight of his warm brown eyes staring out at me took me back to the night at the hotel door.

The CD rode with me in the passenger seat as I hit the Turnpike entrance. I let it sit there until I hit the Blue Mountain Tunnels. I kept glancing over at it, working up the nerve to put it in my player. As I emerged from the tunnel, I quickly grabbed it and advanced it to track 7. Cruising down the empty Turnpike in the dead of night, Joshua began to sing. It was a song that was every bit of pain I had shared with him; how it hurt to breathe, how living without someone you love can tear you apart, but how in the end…it all ends up as it should be. Our brief affair and final moments set into melody.

The track ended and I drove for many miles in complete silence. I was alone in the car, and then I wasn't. As the snow began to fall, I looked over and Camille sat in the passenger seat.

Just drive with me for a while, Camille. Just stay with me a little longer.

We drove together on our last adventure down the Turnpike. As the signs gave me a prompt that the exit for home was 10 miles away, I turned to her and she gave me that crooked smirk that revealed her dimple.

Oh! It's on the right side, not the left, I thought as I returned my eyes to the road.

My turn signal blinked, tick...tick...to mark my sharp right-hand turn to get off the exit. When I looked back over to the passenger seat, she was gone. I sighed deeply and pointed my car in the direction it had always been going...to a life that was entirely, sadly, scarily, painfully, excitingly my own.

The snow fell harder now, making the road ahead harder to see. Fitting, I thought. The path forward never was clear. For so long, I'd looked at my life and thought, "This is not my life." But somewhere between grief and survival, between questions without answers and a truth no one wanted to name, it had become mine.

As each unique and individual snowflake created a solid blanket of snow covering my path home, I realized they were all in that car with me, inside of me. My dad's anger, my mom's love for beautiful things, the children's resilience, Jillian's faith, Alan's humor, Sean's loyalty, Joshua's longing for more, and most of all Camille's fight to live every moment she had, like the ride would be wild but short.

Tick. Tick.

This is my life. Not defined by the loss of those I loved, but created from the pieces of life they gave me. I am, most of all, the sister who was left behind to steer the way into a new, unknown direction with her fingers tightly wrapped around the wheel and hovering above a keyboard to tell the tale.

Acknowledgments

I cannot begin to thank people without first giving gratitude to Erin Donley. This book would have remained buried like the unheard songs inside my piano bench without her enthusiastic support and guidance through the publishing process.

To my boys, Evan and Seth – Thank you for always understanding that your mom went through a time when she drifted off into sadness. You were both the reason I fought to find my way back home.

Lastly, to my sister's children, David, Alec and Diana – Your mom loved you. I love you. Thank you for growing up to be superheroes.